W9-AYE-644
FORT WORTH PUBLIC LIBRARY

3 1668 03241 7948

ON MY JOURNEY NOW

CEN   CHILDREN 782.25
   GIOVANNI 2009
Giovanni, Nikki
On my journey now

Central   09/10/2009

CENTRAL LIBRARY

ON MY JOURNEY NOW

◎ ◆ ◎ ◆ ◎

LOOKING AT AFRICAN-AMERICAN HISTORY
THROUGH THE SPIRITUALS

◆ ◆ ◆ ◎ ◆ ◆ ◆

NIKKI GIOVANNI

Foreword by Dr. Arthur C. Jones,
Founder and Artistic Program Director
of the Spirituals Project

Complete Lyrics for the Spirituals Included

CANDLEWICK PRESS

Copyright © 2007 by Nikki Giovanni
Foreword copyright © 2007 by Arthur C. Jones

"Ain't Got Time to Die" by Hall Johnson, copyright © 1955 (renewed)
by G. Schirmer, Inc. (ASCAP) International copyright secured.
All rights reserved. Reprinted by permission.
"Going Up to Glory" by Dr. Andre Thomas. Used by permission of the author.

All rights reserved. No part of this book may be reproduced, transmitted,
or stored in an information retrieval system in any form or by any means,
graphic, electronic, or mechanical, including photocopying, taping, and
recording, without prior written permission from the publisher.

First paperback edition 2009

The Library of Congress has cataloged the hardcover edition as follows:

Giovanni, Nikki.
On my journey now : looking at African-American history through the spirituals
/ Nikki Giovanni ; foreword by Arthur C. Jones. —1st ed.
p.   cm.
"Complete lyrics for the spirituals included."
ISBN 978-0-7636-2885-7 (hardcover)
1. Spirituals (Songs)—History and criticism—Juvenile literature.
2. African Americans—History—Juvenile literature.   I. Title.
PS3557.I55O6 2007
782.25'3—dc22   2006051695

ISBN 978-0-7636-4380-5 (paperback)

2 4 6 8 10 9 7 5 3 1

Printed in the United States of America

This book was typeset in Tiepolo and Baskerville.

Candlewick Press
99 Dover Street
Somerville, Massachusetts 02144

visit us at www.candlewick.com

To the bravery of those African women who, in 1619,

stood on the gangplank of a Dutch man-of-war,

held hands, and courageously walked into the new world

⦿ CONTENTS

"CHANGE IS GOING TO COME"

Nikki Giovanni loves the spirituals—the sacred songs created and first sung by enslaved African peoples in North America in the seventeenth, eighteenth, and nineteenth centuries. For many years, for anyone willing to listen, she has told stories that help listeners understand why the spirituals are so important to her and why they should be important to all of us. She has lamented the veil of ignorance and misunderstanding surrounding the legacy of the spirituals. She has implored her listeners to correct their misunderstandings. She has demanded that they understand.

Countless women and men throughout the decades have written about the spirituals. Activists, scholars, musicians, poets— all have offered their insights. The list of written commentators has included many great names: W. E. B. Du Bois, Zora Neale Hurston, Paul Robeson, James Weldon Johnson, James Cone, Bernice Johnson Reagon, and many others. However, Nikki boldly offers something new and fresh, expanding her intimate listening circle into an infinitely larger but still intimate community of intergenerational readers.

Nikki employs her keen poetic vision to guide us through the inner world of the brave Africans in bondage who created the spirituals, helping us discover for ourselves some of the reasons why today, as much or perhaps more than ever, we need the ancestral wisdom we find when we venture into that world. The insights Nikki offers are profound and unsettling, and they might have been packaged with a warning: Read at your own risk, and be aware that the changes you experience in yourself will make you feel uneasy, but they will be good for you—and for us.

Nikki challenges us to see the spirituals through the eyes of the original singers and their progeny. She raises many questions for us to consider and provides her own personal answers for us to ponder. For example, she asks us to think about why a people in the midst of suffering and trauma would want to sing. She asks us to sit with the idea that the singers were simply proud of their work (even though it was imposed on them) and that they sang as an expression of that pride. This forces us to discard the common image of enslaved people as victims in favor of an image of them as intact human beings, motivated by the same positive forces that have motivated human beings in all times and places throughout the centuries.

In reenvisioning the creators of the spirituals, Nikki also demands that we consider the multiple layers of injustice they experienced and their desperate but powerful response to it, as captured in their moans and—eventually—their songs. She also introduces us to the genius of the singers, seen in so many ways, including their decision to escape from slavery by day rather than by night. The effectiveness of this strategy is reflected in the eagerness to pass fugitive slave laws and in the sheer number of escapees over the years—one hundred thousand, by the South's own estimate.

Nobody knows specifically when or where particular spirituals were created and sung. Rather than speculate on this, Nikki simply points out the universal meanings of songs and how they illustrate the challenges that enslaved Africans faced in dealing with their captors. She quotes "Done Made My Vow," for example, to help us picture the horrors experienced by the Africans thrown into the holds of slave ships during the Middle Passage. Throughout the book, Nikki encourages us to understand the experiences of people in bondage by immersing ourselves in the lyrics, melodies, and rhythms of the songs they have passed on to us. Her approach lends new meaning to songs like "This Little Light of Mine," "Kumbaya," "All God's Children," "Sometimes I Feel Like a Motherless Child," and many other spirituals that have previously been thought about in less creative ways.

If we as mothers, fathers, daughters, and sons follow Nikki's guidance, we are guaranteed to be touched by the infinite wisdom that comes through these songs we call spirituals. This is fortunate, because God knows, we need that wisdom.

Arthur C. Jones, PhD
Founder and Artistic Program Director of the Spirituals Project

◎◆◎◆◎ THE JOURNEY ◎◆◎◆◎

On my journey now, Mount Zion.
Well, I wouldn't take nothing, Mount Zion,
For my journey now, Mount Zion.

One day, one day, I was walking along,
Well, the elements opened and the love
come down, Mount Zion.

These are the questions: How did the enslaved Africans live through the brutal period of the Middle Passage—that frightening time of capture, forced march to the African west coast, being put down in places like Cape Coast Castle or Gorée Island (like so many cows or horses or any number of life forces human beings pen up)—and come to this newly invented nation sane?

Sane is an important word because the captured had to know there was an insanity controlling their destiny. They saw the old beaten down; they saw the infants bayoneted; they felt the heat of villages being burned; they heard the growling of wild animals that followed the shackled to devour those who could not keep up.

Sane is important because no sane person would invest in a business on the verge of bankruptcy. And America, while extolling the rights of man in language more fluid and forceful than ever before was, because of the slavery of Africans and the genocide of Native Americans, along with a failure to heed the advice of Abigail Adams to "remember the ladies," on the verge of moral bankruptcy.

Yet the captured came to this nation, surveyed this moral landscape, recognized the valleys as well as the hills, and deposited their dreams right here. Stepping off the ships to a language that demeaned them, to a topography totally unfamiliar, to a God they did not know, they nonetheless found a way to laugh, love, and believe in tomorrow.

It has been a long journey. And these brave African people have joined hands with all other Americans to continue climbing Jacob's ladder. We are all on a journey now, to the unknown where the rights of all people, all animals, all flora are respected. It is a journey now to protect the different, the weak, the needy, the hurt, the abused. It is a journey now that we all continue to work to discover the best of the American dream of freedom.

> *I went to the valley and I didn't go to stay.*
> *Well, my soul got happy and I stayed all day,*
>   *Mount Zion.*
>
> *Just talk about me, just as much as you please.*
> *Well, I'll talk about you when I bend my knees,*
>   *Mount Zion.*

◎◆◎◆◎ SLAVERY ◎◆◎◆◎

We say that the slavers went to Africa to get the slaves, which is far from true. The slavers went to Africa to get the Africans to make them slaves. These were free people. These were people with their own cultures, their own families, their own relationships, their own ways of doing things, their own food-stuffs, their own clothes, their own everything, and they were ripped away from their homelands. Overpowered. These people were a brave people. And I think it's so easy to forget that they had choices. I am a big fan of the American Indians, the Native Americans, because they said, "No, I don't think I'll be a slave in my own land."

America was looking for very, very, very cheap labor, because they wanted workers who were even cheaper than indentured servants. The Africans were taken from their homes, their villages, their cities. They were chained and lined up, and people who could not keep up were thrown to the side. So many people dying changed the patterns of the pred-ators, especially the hyenas, the buzzards, the scavengers. The animals came in closer to the coast, following their prey.

The slavers took the Africans to places like Cape Coast Castle and Gorée Island, where they were put down under. I've had the privilege of actually visiting Cape Coast Castle and Gorée Island and also Dachau, the site of a Nazi concen-tration camp. When I was in Dachau, I smelled the gas. As you traveled through, you could smell the gas. And in the dungeons where they were holding the Africans to take them to America to make them slaves, you could hear the moans. I was talking to the singer Roberta Flack at one point, and she said, "Did you, girl? Did you hear it?" And I said, "Ro, I did." I mean, you feel it. It's there. It's a sort of a moan.

◎◆◎◆◎ THE MOAN ◎◆◎◆◎

They rowed these people out to the sailboats that were going to take them to America. When they put people on ships—and it was deliberate—they separated family groups so they could not speak to each other, so they could not plot. So the slavers had these people on their hands who they had to keep healthy-looking, or else they weren't going to get anything for them. Sometimes they had to force them to eat, because some of them would go on hunger strikes. They were packed head to toe in the ship. Anything that came out of the next person fell on you. So the sailors had to bring you up and pour water on you to more or less wash you. It's not a wash, but it does what it is supposed to do; it gets off all the dirt and mess that is covering you.

We know from the diaries of slave captains that if they brought the Africans up the first or second day, they would jump overboard because the people could just look back and see home. And, having seen it, having recognized that this was not really going to be a good idea at all, and having struggled, they would want to go back. There is something I'm always laughing about: the myth that Africans don't swim, which is crazy. When swimming pools were segregated, that made it harder for African Americans to learn to swim. But of course Africans could swim; many lived near the Atlantic Ocean, and they would swim. In some cases when they jumped overboard, they were shot in the back and wounded and they died, and in other cases they made it. Most ended up in the belly of a shark. The sharks, too, changed their patterns. They began to follow the ships west, feeding on the bodies of the dead or dying Africans.

So the slavers waited, got to that fourth and fifth day, and then there was a calm among the Africans, and they talked about that. There was a calm because they could look out, and although they couldn't see the land, they could see the heat coming off the land. They could see that shimmer, and it's the most fantastic thing to travel to Africa by boat, because you see the heat before you see the land.

And so, by that sixth or seventh day, or maybe around the eighth day, they could no longer see the land or the heat, and so there is going to be a restlessness, because people are beginning to feel lost, because now they're thinking, "Well, this is farther out." So now we have the Africans in a position of not really being able to see anything familiar. But of course they followed the clouds, and we do know that clouds above land are different from clouds over water, so they could see that land had to be *that* way. And so we're going to have a serious problem somewhere around the tenth day. And those who study this—I'm just a poet, but the people who study slavery— say that those ships' captains knew that this was going to be the day that, I don't want to say all hell is going to break loose, but the day they really have to tighten up, because now the people realize they will not know how to get home.

Fare you well, fare you well, fare you well, everybody.
Fare you well, fare you well, whenever I do get a-home.

What those captured people had—which is why I so admire those people—was a tone, a voice, a moan. They made a decision, because they had to decide: Do we shut ourselves down, or do we continue forward? Now, they ultimately are going to sing a lot of songs; they're going to sing a song that says,

Done made my vow to the Lord,
And I never will turn back.
I will go,
I shall go,
To see what the end will be.

Done opened my mouth to the Lord,
And I never will turn back.
I will go,
I shall go,
To see what the end will be.

So, it's a fabulous thing. But there is also a much sadder song that says,

I told Jesus it would be all right if He changed my name,
I told Jesus it would be all right if He changed my name,
I told Jesus it would be all right if He changed my name.

And He told me that I would go hungry if He changed my
   name,
And He told me that I would go hungry if He changed my
   name,
And He told me that I would go hungry if He changed my
   name.

The Africans are trying to decide, do we continue forward to see what the end will be, or not? Do we agree to
change our names, or not? And frankly speaking, I always
think it was a woman who started the singing, because I think
women do that. Somewhere in the belly of that ship, a woman
started in humming, because she couldn't call out and speak
to others—there were too many different languages. But she
could hum, and that hum, that moan was picked up and went
all over the ship and became a single voice. We've heard it in
groups like the Moses Hogan Chorale; you hear the voices of
all of those people becoming one voice, and it's a moan. But
that moan says, "We will find a way; we will continue."

◎•◎•◎ WE WILL CONTINUE ◎•◎•◎

The people had to find a way to say, "This is who I am." Ultimately they are going to find a way to say that, and they are going to say to each other and to their children, "If anybody asks you who you are, tell them you are a child of God. Never, never tell them you are a slave. Never, never tell them you belong to 'Masser.' Tell them you are a child of God." It's an amazing, amazing thing to me that she—because I have to think it was a she—found that tone.

> *If anybody asks you who I am, who I am, who I am,*
> *If anybody asks you who I am,*
> *Tell them I'm a child of God.*

We do know that mothers who sing to their children have quieter children, have children who are calmer. And by being calmer, they are more able to be instructed. A mother recognizes that if she can hum a child to sleep, she is going to be able to teach that child the ways of the community and the child is not going to be agitated. Agitated children cannot learn. (It would be better today if we were able to hold children who are crying and rock them and just hum some little lullaby for them. We know that they would, in fact, sleep better, that they would rest better. A bowl of grits with butter, maybe a piece of toast and a glass of milk before school, not to mention a good hot bowl of pinto beans with a piece of fatback and some cold-water corn bread at lunch would help, too.)

The moan on the ship calmed fears; it allowed people to come into another world and prepare for what everybody had to know was going to be unpleasant. They always say that the slaves didn't know what they were getting into and what it meant when they were captured. The captured did know that these people were not nice people, that these people were mean, and that these people had no good offices to offer.

When the captured people came into the Caribbean, into Barbados, into Baltimore, when they came into those ports, they were put on auction blocks, which they stood on naked. I think that is so important for people to recognize: that you stood on those blocks. They oiled you up and they put you on those auction blocks and you were naked, and people came and put their hands all over you to see if they were going to purchase you. And then they did purchase you, branded you, chained you, and walked you to a plantation.

It's always been an amazement to me that America has anything critical to say about the black family, because the black family had to be re-created, and it was being re-created out of people whose only thing in common was that they were purchased by a particular person. If it were easy to do, prisons would have families; they would find a way, because that, too, is an artificial situation. We have to give the captured credit for being able to find a way to communicate in a language they had never heard of, with a religion that was totally new, in a land they knew they would not return from. Whatever dreams they had now would have to be deposited in American soil, and that they did that is again such a fantastic thing.

There is a story that Maxine Hong Kingston tells in *China Men* about the cruelty the Chinese workers suffered on the pineapple plantations in Hawaii. The men, on their day of rest, would go to a certain spot, dig a hole, and whisper their stories into the ground, hoping the stories would find their way back to China. The dreams of the Africans made slaves were deposited in the soil of the American Dream— which is, perhaps, why Martin Luther King's greatest speech was the one where he described that dream to the nation, and to the world.

As sad as slavery was going to be, it was also an opportunity for the people to imagine new lives. Phillis Wheatley was an enslaved woman in the 1700s who gained a reputation around the world for her poetry. She wrote that she was angry with those who sold her as well as with those who bought her. And despite being bought and sold, she had to find a way to thrive. It was a strange thing for the Africans now in America. Where they now lived was their home, which they came to love as their home. But it was also a plantation where they were owned. It was a place where they could leave behind bad things from the past, where they could be reborn. And yet it was their prison.

◎✦◎✦◎ A SLAVE'S DAY ◎✦◎✦◎

Nobody gives these people credit for the work they did in building America. They paced themselves with work songs. And the overseer who was stupid would say things like, "I don't want them singing, because I don't know what they are saying," because they were singing in a native language. But of course what it did was create the work rhythm, and you might say, "Well, what did they care?" Why should they sing to be able to work better? They recognized that they had to be proud of the work that they did. They didn't have to like the people who were in charge, because there was nothing to like about these people. They knew that this was not a good situation, but if they could find a way to take pride in the work of their hands, they could do something that few people have done in this world: they could remain sane. To toil for a higher master was a great, great covenant.

Imagine a slave's day: They get up a little bit before dawn—at five o'clock or five thirty. They have grits or whatever it is the old ladies who can no longer work in the field are cooking, and they are in the field at six o'clock, when dawn is coming up. And they would have you picking cotton or whatever it was you were doing. This changed once we went to sharecropping. The cotton is wet at that hour in the morning and it is heavier, so you would not pick it when it was wet; you would wait. But then you'd go out to the field and you'd work. By the time the sun comes up at eight or nine o'clock— we're talking Mississippi, Alabama, and Georgia—it's hot.

Water boy, where are you hiding?
If you don't come right here,
I'm gonna tell your pa on you.

They found a way not to make a joke of it, but to make something lovely. They found a way to sing. They knew that there were many, many, many things they could not say, but they could call for the water boy. And the water boy could hear that tone, and he could say, "Well, I'm the water boy. I'm not a slave; I'm a part of the workforce."

The same way you and I would say, "I went to work with my mother," or "I went to the office with Dad today," they were in the fields saying, "I'm a water boy. This is who I am, and I will take pride in that." It's so lovely.

They stopped for lunch, of course, and I'm sure they were pretty tired, but then they worked until sundown. We sing that song:

Sunup to sundown, picking that cotton;
Sunup to sundown, work for the master;
Sunup to sundown, chains and shackles;
No more auction block for me.

And that is what they did: work from sunup to sundown. When they were done, they came home, and before they had dinner, they washed. Many of them were Muslims. Just because they were enslaved didn't mean they were uncivilized; they washed. And maybe the shirt was ragged, maybe the shirt didn't fit right, but they changed and put on clean clothes.

They washed their hands, they sat down, and they sang another song:

Let us break bread together on our knees (on our knees),
Let us break bread together on our knees (on our knees).
When I fall on my knees with my face to the rising sun,
O Lord, have mercy on me.

The rising sun is in the east, and as we know, Muslims are required to pray to the east. There is nothing in the Christian religion nor, I believe, any other that requires that you face west. But the Muslims are required to face east and pray. They are required to pray five times a day. I am a Christian, and I need to learn more about other religions, but I've always been fascinated by the words, "When I fall on my knees with my face to the rising sun," because they could not have fallen on their knees with their faces to the rising sun, because they were in the field before the sun was rising. So it means that somehow somebody remembered something, despite it all—and that's what is so interesting—and held it close and found a way to deposit it.

The only way that we are going to deposit any of these things is going to be through a song, because the enslaved are not allowed to read. We were not allowed to write; being able to read and write was actually a reason to be sold away from everybody that you knew, which might have happened anyway, but that was certainly one of the major reasons. If you could read or write, you were definitely going to be, first of all, whipped very badly and, second, most likely just sold away, because nobody could take a chance on your doing things like writing passes, which they did. We have wonderful stories of people writing passes on the Underground Railroad.

It must have been women who wrote those passes, because they had the chance to trace, to copy out, the handwriting of the young mistresses. It was much harder for a man to learn to write, and certainly to do so with the kind of polish that could fool someone. (Of course, there is the story of Henry "Box" Brown, who instead of just writing a pass, addressed a label and had a collaborator box him up and mail him to freedom.)

◎◆◎◆◎ ESCAPE ◎◆◎◆◎

The enslaved ran away. There was a bleeding of the South, just a bleeding of the South.

Follow the drinking gourd!
Follow the drinking gourd,
For the old man is a-waiting for to carry you to freedom
If you follow the drinking gourd.

When the sun comes back and the first quail calls,
Follow the drinking gourd,
For the old man is a-waiting for to carry you to freedom
If you follow the drinking gourd.

The riverbank makes a very good road;
The dead trees will show you the way.
Left foot, peg foot traveling on,
Following the drinking gourd.

It makes me so unhappy to see black kids not in love with the stars. I don't see how you can be a black youngster and not just spend all of your time looking at the heavens. We are the people who built the Great Pyramid of Giza. We did high math there. And our ancestors followed the drinking gourd, the Big Dipper, which, if you are in, say, Florida, looks a little bit different from the way it looks farther north. But they did that. They knew how to follow the moss on the north side of the trees. Who was teaching all this? Nobody was holding classes on how to be a runaway slave. How were they learning these things? They were learning these things through songs.

Harriet Tubman came down South again and again to lead people to freedom. It was so wonderful. Her song was:

'Tis the old ship of Zion,
'Tis the old ship of Zion,
'Tis the old ship of Zion.
Get on board! Get on board!

She could preach that. The overseer could hear her singing and not put two and two together. The overseers didn't hang out with each other and say, "Oh, did your slave sing some song, 'The Old Ship of Zion'?" But the slaves knew what it meant, and they would say, "Moses is here. Moses is here." I have to think that "Go Down, Moses" is definitely about Tubman, although it would not have been Tubman's song.

Tubman was not the only conductor on the Underground Railroad, but she was the one that slaveholders knew and hated, and they put such a price on her head. She had the equivalent of one hundred thousand dollars or more on her head, so somebody who turned her in would have that much money and freedom, but nobody did. Nobody recognized an old black woman. During the Civil War, she fought to be a spy for the Union, then later she had to fight the government to receive her pension. She died of old age on her porch in upstate New York.

I've always been interested in the Underground Railroad. I'm proud of the Quakers, and I think that it was a wonderful thing that they shared our love of freedom and opened up their homes to us. Quakers actually were arrested and sent to jail, as were European Catholics in World War II who were kind enough to take in Jewish kids and families. You know, we've always had situations like that. But you had to set off running by yourself, and nobody wants to give us credit for doing that.

Once a person set foot off their plantation, how did they get around? I'm a wildlife person. The expression that the rangers always use is "A fed bear is a dead bear." I'm from Knoxville, Tennessee, and we used to spend time in the Smoky Mountains. You cannot feed the bears there, because if you feed them, they get used to it and get used to humans.

A black man at night on the road was a dead man. If you were running at night, you were dead, because you would be caught. There were too many dogs. The only way to run was during the day, which is another fascinating thing about the Underground Railroad. The only real way to escape was plantation to plantation, because most plantations weren't all that big. The average plantation had only fifty or sixty slaves, but the masters didn't really know what they looked like. You know, there is always this joke, and it makes sense to me: If you want to be a bank robber, what is the best thing to do? Don't bathe! The best thing is don't bathe for like a week or so, so that you have a bit of body odor. And then you get in a wheelchair, and then you just roll the wheelchair in and you have your gun and you rob the bank and you roll it out, right? Nobody will be able to describe you, because people automatically turn away from the afflicted. That's the truth; that is the truth.

When you think about escape, you have to think about men and women walking away in the daytime. It would take courage to try to escape in the evening; it would take courage to run at all. But realize that you had to do it in the daytime. You had to do it when the patrollers were out there and they were saying, "Where you goin', boy?" and you're hanging your head and saying, "I'm going to Masser; Masser sending me to so-and-so." You've got to have your story, you've got to make sure you have the right demeanor, and you have to go from one plantation to the next plantation. You also have to depend on the other slaves.

We know that our good friends the Quakers helped make quilts, and they would hang the quilts out. But who taught the slaves to read the quilts? So the "crazy quilt" said, "Be careful; don't come straight." We are talking, then, about something that nobody acknowledges; we're talking about daytime movement, because you sure as heck can't read a quilt in the middle of the night. Those quilts were hanging out in the daytime when those slaves were moving about as slaves. The key was that you had to maintain.

You had to make sure not to show that you were running. Instead, you had to portray yourself as a slave. And you had to maintain that cool when you were stopped, that demeanor that said, "I belong to somebody." What an acting job you had to do in order to maintain, because if you sweated, you had a problem; if you had an issue with people looking at you, you were in trouble.

How many times do you think the overseer looked at Harriet Tubman? He didn't know who she was, but he was looking at another escaped slave and asking, "Do I know this man?" The person on the run had to work. You move and you work and you're out in the field. The overseer asks, "Who is that?" Someone answers, "Oh, Masser, that's John; you remember John." Nobody turned those people in. Some were caught, but the number was highly disproportionate to those who escaped. The South admits it lost one hundred thousand slaves. That's a lot of people to walk away.

The Fugitive Slave Act is a testament to how many slaves ran away. If the slaves were "happy"—as the masters claimed—then the few malcontents would have been meaningless. No. The slaves were looking to get away, and the South, through the Fugitive Slave Act, made all Americans slaveholders to perpetuate this evil system.

We in the black community are always being told that we cannot depend upon each other, that we will sell each other out for a pork chop or a ham bone. And yet one hundred thousand people went from Mississippi, Alabama, Georgia, Louisiana, and, of course, the easy ones—North Carolina, South Carolina (South Carolina especially, because you went by water, and you had friends who helped you do that), and Maryland.

But think about coming from Louisiana. Because now you're not trying to go north; you're actually trying to go south. You're actually trying to make it back to some place like Haiti, and this is one of the reasons the United States still hates Haiti: because it was a haven. And you could get to Haiti just as you can now, and you could get to Cuba just as you can now; you could get away. You'd have to choose which way you were going, and of course in Florida they just went to the Seminoles. And the Seminole Nation and black Americans intermarried.

The people who stayed, who did not run away, had to find a community, had to find a way to live. After they ate, after they washed, they prayed and cleaned up after themselves— you cleaned up after you washed the dishes and put them away. The slave cabins were not nice. Nobody would say, "Oh, this is really a lovely cabin." But those little cabins stayed clean; they stayed free of mice and vermin and roaches. They had little rugs to sleep on, which again must have been familiar to some from their lives in Africa. After all that, they were tired. They worked from sunup to sundown. They were tired, but they did not go to bed. Instead, they brought whatever they had—a pot for a drum; they could make a flute out of wood; a comb for a mouth harp—they brought what they had, and they made music. The music was invigorating.

I know if I am driving from where I live in Virginia over to Washington, D.C., I am going to put some music on. Because if I don't have it on, I'm going to fall asleep behind the wheel. Music invigorates us, and so for an hour or so they made music and told their troubles to the Lord.

I have to think, when they sang in the evening, if it was

I'm trampin', trampin',
Trying to make heaven my home;
I'm trampin', trampin',
Trying to make heaven my home;

I'm trampin', trampin',
Trying to make heaven my home;
I'm trampin', trampin',
Trying to make heaven my home,

that meant there was a slave on the move, and he was saying to somebody, "Yes, this is who I am, so take care of me." And they did. He was saying, "Don't punk me out"—not using those words, but they had to have a way of saying, "Who is here?" Everybody would know that something was going on—that someone was on the move.

You get these songs saying,

Hush, hush, somebody's calling my name,
Hush, hush, somebody's calling my name,
Hush, hush, somebody's calling my name,
O my Lord, O my Lord, what shall I do?

Their situation was terrible, but again the genius and the strength of these people is that they didn't look at it; they didn't look at the bigger picture. They were thinking, "I'm going to deal with today's problem today, because that's all I can handle." And then you had "those kind" of days: your wife was sold, your husband was sold, your baby died. That would make you sing, "Been in the Storm So Long."

I've been in the storm so long,
You know I've been in the storm so long,

I've been in the storm so long,
O Lord, give me more time to pray.

I am a motherless child,
Singing, I am a motherless child,
I've been in the storm so long,
O Lord, give me more time to pray.

The slave community was not a judgmental community. It's not going to become judgmental until we get to Emancipation, because the slave community is going to let you do what you have to do. If you had the baby and it lived, if you had the baby and it died, they were not going to judge you. And I could see why. Anything you do is a bad decision, because you can't protect your child, you know. You know that when she is twelve years old she is going to be a really pretty girl, so the master's brother, cousin, whatever is going to be all over her, and it had to be a bad decision. It had to be a bad decision. Yes, "been in the storm so long."

We usually sing "This Little Light of Mine" as a happy song:

This little light of mine,
I'm gonna let it shine.
This little light of mine,
I'm gonna let it shine.
This little light of mine,
I'm gonna let it shine,

Let it shine,
Let it shine,
Let it shine!

But there is another way to do it. Kathleen Battle sings it as a demand: "This little light of mine, / I'm going to let it shine." It's not a happy song; it's that I *am* going to live.

◎◆◎◆◎ SUNDAY ◎◆◎◆◎

Every day was the same to the slaves. They had no sense of a week, a month, even a year. They saw the masters act differently on some days, but that did not change their lives. A rainy day was a good day, because it meant you did not have to go out into the cotton fields or the tobacco fields. But they had no punctuation to their lives except night and day, day and night.

In the middle to late 1700s, preachers began to speak to black and white congregations in the South, and the masters could no longer prevent people from becoming Christians. Phillis Wheatley wrote,

> *Some view our sable race with scornful eye,*
> *"Their colour is a diabolic die."*
> *Remember, Christians, Negroes, black as Cain,*
> *May be refin'd, and join th' angelic train.*

Now Sunday started to become a different day. That gave the people a way of counting off, going through the week until Sunday came again. During the day they could praise God; they had something of their own.

> *Jesus calls you. Go in the wilderness,*
> *Go in the wilderness, go in the wilderness.*
> *Jesus calls you. Go in the wilderness*
> *To wait upon the Lord.*

Go wait upon the Lord,
Go wait upon the Lord,
Go wait upon the Lord, my God.
He takes away the sins of the world.

Now, the enslaved did indeed go into the wilderness to hold church meetings. I would bet nobody ever ran away at these meetings, because the slaveholders would have killed not just that particular group but all the rest. It had to be so confusing to white people that the blacks were out there and all they were doing was singing these songs, and the whites didn't like it but couldn't say no. The slaves would say, "We just want to worship," and look really humble, so the owners would say, "Well, it's OK; let them worship." And then, while the slaves didn't run away, they gave information to each other; they passed it along, and they taught each other.

◎◆◎◆◎ IF YOU WANT RELIGION ◎◆◎◆◎

"If You Want Religion"—we sang that during the civil rights movement. The leader would call out, "If you want religion," and we'd respond, "go in the wilderness." I sing it too fast, because it's in march time, but of course it's so wonderful because it helped you to teach. And the Bible has been a great teaching tool. There are still people in the United States whose only goal—I mean older people in their eighties and nineties—who say, "Before I die, I want to know how to read the Bible; I want to know how to write my name," and of course it used to be, "I want to vote." But now those people can vote, and it's such a wonderful thing. In the wilderness they heard the Bible stories, and they passed them on.

The Jews were enslaved in Egypt, but God freed them. That was a story of hope, but also of warning:

Go down, Moses,
'Way down in Egypt's land,
Tell old Pharaoh,
To let my people go.

When the Jews arrived in the Promised Land, they had to fight to hold it. Again, God was with them.

Joshua fit the battle of Jericho,
Jericho, Jericho.

Joshua fit the battle of Jericho,
And the walls come tumbling down.

In some of the Old Testament songs you hear the beginnings of hope. I don't mean to overstate hope, because there was no tunnel, there was no light at the end of this tunnel, even when we come down from 1619, when the first slaves were brought to Virginia, to the 1760s, when the Revolutionary War was imminent. House slaves were passing the word that the United States and England were going to go to war. And once the fighting began, England made an offer: fight with us, and we'll help you get freedom.

The Americans talked about freedom, and the slaves sang:

Didn't my Lord deliver Daniel,
Deliver Daniel, deliver Daniel,
Didn't my Lord deliver Daniel,
And why not every man?

The Americans said they were fighting for freedom, for liberty. And the song says, "And why not every man?" But the Americans had no intention of freeing their slaves, and they didn't. That was a big mistake, because they missed a wonderful opportunity to resolve this thing a little more amicably.

Now that the slaves were Christians, they learned the Bible stories. So, we had the whole Old Testament.

Wheel, oh, wheel,
Wheel in the middle of a wheel;
Wheel, oh, wheel,
Wheel in the middle of a wheel.

Ezekiel saw the wheel of time,
Wheel in the middle of a wheel.
Every spoke was humankind,
Wheel in the middle of a wheel.

This was a creation story, about all God's children, all spokes on the wheel of humankind.

There are two songs that are treated as children's songs but were never intended that way. One is "Kumbaya." This is a Gullah song from the sea islands off of Georgia. Gullah is English mixed with many African languages. The word *kumbaya* means "come by here." "Kumbaya, Lord"—everybody sings it in camp and sways and says, "Oh, isn't that cute!" But the song is a petition to God. The enslaved are petitioning God: "Lord, You need to come by here. You need to come see about me."

In the 1960s, the Supremes recorded their own version of "Come See About Me"—but that was flirtatious. The slave song was different. It was, "Lord, You need to come here because these people are not treating me right."

Kumbaya, my Lord, kumbaya,
Kumbaya, my Lord, kumbaya,

Kumbaya, my Lord, kumbaya,
O Lord, kumbaya.

The other song that everybody sings is:

He's got the whole world in His hands,
He's got the whole world in His hands,
He's got the whole world in His hands,
He's got the whole world in His hands.

He's got the wind and the rain in His hands,
He's got the wind and the rain in His hands,
He's got the wind and the rain in His hands,
He's got the whole world in His hands.

We sing that as a children's song instead of looking at it as: "Wait a minute, we are brothers and sisters under the sun, we are worshipping many faces of God, and He's got us all in His hands. So why don't we behave? Why don't we treat each other better?"

The Bible is the language that they have. They are hearing the Old Testament in church and applying it to their own lives. They even used the Bible stories to teach what the masters did not want them to know. How do you teach numbers to little children?

Children, go where I send thee.
How will I send thee?

I'm a-going to send thee
Twelve by twelve,
Twelve as the twelve apostles,
Eleven as the eleven disciples,
Ten as the Ten Commandments,
Nine as the nine who never went behind,
Eight as the eight who stood at the gates,
Seven as the seven who went up in heaven,
Six as the six who never got fixed,
Five as the five Gospel preachers,
Four as the four who stood at the door,
Three as the Hebrew children,
Two as Paul and Silas,
One as the little baby born, born, born in Bethlehem.

Knowing numbers was especially important as slavery ended. When the former slaves became sharecroppers, everyone tried to cheat them. But at least they knew how to count. The songs taught them.

◎◆◎◆◎ TALKING ABOUT HEAVEN ◎◆◎◆◎

In the 1960s, some radicals and militants criticized the preachers, the churches, the religious people. They thought Jesus,
acceptance, suffering, nonviolence were weak. Christianity had
just served to keep blacks quiet. But without Jesus, without
religion, the slaves wouldn't have had that one day off. And
what would Nat Turner have done if he couldn't have been a
preacher? How would he have called his men? How would he
have brought them together? Nat Turner was a man not just
of rebellion but of vengeance. He was out to stop the evil of
slavery. No one was listening, and so he determined that God
deserved an army. He formed an army to kill the planters. He
had no hope of actually killing them all. He did not imagine
he would win. But he would act. He would scare them.
He would fight back. Nat Turner was a soldier and a vision-
ary. And he had a song, too. His song was "Steal Away":

> *Steal away, steal away, steal away to Jesus!*
> *Steal away, steal away home,*
> *I ain't got long to stay here.*

When I say the black community did not judge, that
doesn't mean they were polite and quiet. People talked about
other people, because people have always talked about people. I
mean, no matter where you are, somebody is going to say that
you are worse than they are. "Yes, I murdered twelve people,
but he murdered thirteen and cut their fingers off." There is

always going to be somebody else who is worse than you. So they laughed.

Well, I met my sister the other day,
Give her my right hand.
Just as soon as ever my back was turned,
She took and scandalized my name.
Do you call that a sister?
No, no! You call that a sister?
No, no! Scandalized my name.

Well, I met my brother the other day,
Give him my right hand.
Just as soon as ever my back was turned,
He took and scandalized my name.
Do you call that a brother?
No, no! You call that a brother?
No, no! Scandalized my name.

Well, I met my preacher the other day,
Give him my right hand.
Just as soon as ever my back was turned,
He took and scandalized my name.
Do you call that a preacher?
No, no! You call that a preacher?
No, no! Scandalized my name.

This song made everybody laugh, and it still does today. When you had Sunday and services, you also began to have

Saturday night. This is one of those Saturday-night, have-fun songs. This is a call-and-response. For people who did not read, there were only two ways to teach them a song. One was called "lining out," where the preacher sings a line, and everyone sings it back to him. That is how you learn new words.

Here is how a preacher might teach the hymn, "When I Can Read My Title Clear":

When I can read my title clear

        When I can read my title clear

to mansions in the skies,

        to mansions in the skies,

I bid farewell to every fear

        I bid farewell to every fear

and wipe my weeping eyes,

        and wipe my weeping eyes,

And wipe my weeping eyes,

        And wipe my weeping eyes,

and wipe my weeping eyes.

        and wipe my weeping eyes.

I bid farewell to every fear

        I bid farewell to every fear

and wipe my weeping eyes.

        and wipe my weeping eyes.

But with call-and-response, the preacher gives one line that everyone knows, and they answer back. In the civil rights movement we'd sing:

CALL: *Ain't gonna let nobody*
RESPONSE: *Turn me 'round.*
CALL: *Ain't gonna let nobody*
RESPONSE: *Turn me 'round.*
CALL: *Keep on walking,*
RESPONSE: *Keep on talking,*
CALL: *Going up*
RESPONSE: *To Canaan's land.*

In "Scandalized My Name," when she says "my sister," I don't think that is her mother's child. I think that is another woman. "Just as soon as ever my back was turned / . . . Do you call that a sister? / No, no!"—that is a lot of fun.

People talk. You are going to get a lot of, "Are you really baptized?" or "Did you do what you said you were going to do?" and "Aren't you still a sinner?" When I say not judgmental, I mean you don't turn your back on people because of actions that they take. When people came out of slavery, there was going to be a real problem with liaisons, particularly between white men and black women, because the community assumed now that black women had choices, and they did not approve of a liaison. Because her brothers will say, "Well, if I were lying with a white woman, they would kill me, and you are doing this!"

I think during slavery we understood that people make decisions that other people think are choices but are not really choices. You do the best you can do with what you have got in front of you. Nobody has an ideal choice between driving a

Cadillac and walking. That is not a choice. That is a no-brainer. You put bread on the table however you have to, and if you put it there because you work on your back, then you work on your back and you still get up on Sunday morning and go to church. The good church sisters will then talk about you, but that is not what Jesus did. Jesus went to the women at the well, and He talked to them. And everybody said, "How come Jesus is hanging around with the women at the well?" Because that is who needed Him.

What He said to the rich man, to Nicodemus, was "You must be born again. Nicodemus, you are useless. Don't come sneaking up telling Me you believe in Me and you know who I am, you know. You are useless. You must be born again." And so Nicodemus said, "Well, you know, how would I do that? Shall I crawl back in my mother?" And Jesus said, "By the blood and by the water, you must be born again. You need to get a life, Nicodemus."

The slaves said,

I got a robe, you got a robe,
All God's children got a robe.
When I get to Heaven I'm going to put on my robe,
I'm going to shout all over God's Heaven.

Heaven, Heaven,
Everybody talking 'bout Heaven ain't going there;
Heaven, Heaven,
I'm going to shout all over God's Heaven.

They didn't say all God's straight children; they didn't say all God's black children, white children. They said all God's children got a robe. And when I get to Heaven, I'm going to put on the robe and walk all over God's Heaven. "Everybody talking 'bout Heaven ain't going there." And everybody trying to act self-righteous, they are not necessarily on any fast track to the Lord, either. People have a right to live their own lives.

These songs were helping to tell the story, and they were teaching. They were teaching not just the Bible, because the Bible is a good and comforting book, and nothing has distressed me personally as much as the Right Wing taking over a really good book that contains good stories that people learned from and using it as a weapon. The question is not "WWJD"—what would Jesus do? I ask "WDJD"—what *did* Jesus do? And the first thing He did was He turned water into wine. That was a good idea. He was a person you could talk to. And today people are trying to take away that sense of wonder, that sense of compassion.

◎◆◎◆◎ CLIMBING ◎◆◎◆◎

The largest slave uprising before the American Revolution took place in Stono, South Carolina, in 1739. Because the owners feared that the slaves were using drums to communicate, drums were often banned in parts of the South. The Africans did use drums to "speak" to each other.

It has been maybe thirty-five years now since the first time I went to Africa. I was in Swaziland, and my driver picked me up at the airport and stopped at one point. Swaziland is beautiful—it is so beautiful. He stopped at one point and said, "Do you hear that?" It was a drum. I said, "Yes; drums." He said "Yeah," and he was really pleased. "Do you know what they are saying?" I said, "No; do you?" And he said, "They are saying that the American poet is on her way, that you have been picked up." I said, "How do you know that?" And he said, "I can hear; I can hear the drums." I thought it was totally fascinating. And of course they gave me a demonstration, which was Greek to me, and they showed me that when you do this, this, and this, and it comes like that, then this is what they are sending.

So, they sent messages. When they were not allowed to drum, they still found other ways to beat the rhythms. They did a circle dance, going counterclockwise. You can picture four or five people, not to mention a whole community, in the wilderness with their feet hitting the ground together, and that's going to be a kind of drum. It's not going to carry for any particular distance, but it's going to be the Drum, and it's going to carry the beat, and that's going to be important.

Religion worked in another way, too, using the beat and rhythm.

We am climbing
Jacob's ladder,
We am climbing
Jacob's ladder,
We am climbing
Jacob's ladder,
Soldiers of the cross.

Every round goes
Higher, higher,
Every round goes
Higher, higher,
Every round goes
Higher, higher,
Soldiers of the cross.

"Jacob's Ladder" was a ring shout. A ring shout is a round; you start one at a time and end up in the same place.

I grew up in three churches, which is very fortunate. My mother was AME, African Methodist Episcopal, in Cincinnati. She grew up in the Baptist church. So when I lived with my grandmother, I went to the Baptist church. And when I went to school, I went to an Episcopal school. I have all of these experiences of different ways to sing. I remember "Jacob's

Ladder." We would go to prayer meeting on Wednesday night and sing "Jacob's Ladder." You had to be holding hands; you'd be in a circle, just as in,

Will the circle be unbroken?
By and by, Lord, by and by,
There's a better home a-waiting
In the sky, Lord, in the sky.

You would actually sing yourself into Heaven, into the sky. We're not Holiness, because the Holiness people sing themselves into a faint, and that must be amazing. Like a runner, an athlete, you have endorphins running through your body. You have just taken yourself someplace else. That has to be a relief. Some say that makes you passive. No. Religion, that experience, gives people the ability to stand up and demand change.

Christianity does preach accepting your lot. But it also brings a demand:

Were you there when they crucified my Lord?
Were you there when they crucified my Lord?
Oh! Sometimes it causes me to tremble, tremble, tremble.
Were you there when they crucified my Lord?

"Were You There?" is actually about Nat Turner. It was how the slaves dealt with the fact that Turner had finally been caught. But "tremble" meant more than that. Thomas Jefferson himself wrote, "I tremble for my country when I reflect that God is just." But God is not just; He is merciful. It is nature that is just. It will rain on anyone; it will flood any city.

There was a lot that the people did have to accept. They were punished if they tried to learn to read or write, to educate themselves, or to escape. There were cruel masters, masters coming around after their women—bad, bad, things. But in the songs, they could talk back.

Heaven, Heaven,
Everybody talking 'bout Heaven ain't going there;
Heaven, Heaven,
I'm going to shout all over God's Heaven.

By the 1800s "Masser" didn't mind the singing. He was watching over the slaves working and thinking, "Isn't this sweet? The darkies are singing," without realizing that they were sounding on him; they were signifying; they knew who wasn't going to heaven: they could see him right there.

That was one way the songs worked: double meanings that allowed the people to talk back and yet not get into trouble. But slavery was not a good situation. It was not funny. And the songs showed that.

Lord, I want to be a Christian in my heart, in my heart,
Lord, I want to be a Christian in my heart.
In my heart, in my heart,
Lord, I want to be a Christian in my heart.

This is a song that shows how hard it was. It is saying, "Lord, it is very hard not to hate these people. They are terrible. Help me to be more holy. Help me to be more like Jesus."

Because:

They crucified my Lord,
Not a word, not a word, not a word.
They crucified my Lord,
Not a word, not a word, not a word.
They crucified my Lord,
But He never said a mumbling word,
Not a word, not a word, not a word.

Yes, the slaves are trying to accept what is happening to them; they are trying to be like Jesus. But to accept is not to embrace.

There is another song that I love:

I heard my mother say,
I heard my mother say,
I heard my mother say,
"Give me Jesus."

Give me Jesus,
Give me Jesus.
You may have all this world;
Give me Jesus.

At dark midnight was my cry,
Dark midnight was my cry,
Dark midnight was my cry,
"Give me Jesus."

In the morning when I rise,
In the morning when I rise,
In the morning when I rise,
Give me Jesus.

And when I come to die,
And when I come to die,
And when I come to die,
Give me Jesus.

There are two versions of the song. The other way of singing it is, "You can have all the world; give me Jesus," but that makes no sense to me. Nobody was giving the slaves the world. "You, you others, you may have the world. But when I die, give me Jesus." Jesus was innocent, and He accepted His death. We sinners here, we, too, have to find a way.

Enslaved people also had to find a way to stay alive, to get up in the morning, to work:

Lord, I keep so busy praising my Jesus,
Keep so busy praising my Jesus,
Keep so busy praising my Jesus,
Ain't got time to die.

'Cause when I'm healing the sick,
When I'm healing the sick,
When I'm healing the sick,
I'm praising my Jesus,
Ain't got time to die.

'Cause it takes all of my time,
It takes all of my time,
It takes all of my time,
To praise my Jesus,
Ain't got time to die.

If I don't praise Him,
If I don't praise Him,
If I don't praise Him,
The rocks are going to cry out,
"Glory and honor! Glory and honor!"
Ain't got time to die.

'Cause when I'm feeding the poor,
When I'm feeding the poor,
When I'm feeding the poor,
I'm working for the Kingdom,
Ain't got time to die.

I hear a woman singing this song: "Because when I'm healing the sick, when I'm feeding the poor, you know I'm working for the Kingdom. Now, won't you get out of my way and let me do my work?" Some of these songs clearly were the men's, but this one is the kind of thing that the old ladies could even sing: "Now, won't you get out of my way and let me praise my Jesus, out of my way; if I don't praise Him, the rocks are going to cry out, 'Glory and honor, glory and honor!' Ain't got time to die." This is one of my favorites, because it's a happy song. You go to work in the morning, and you "keep so busy working for the Kingdom."

It is not easy to find that way, that path, that energy. Sometimes it doesn't seem to be there at all.

And I couldn't hear nobody pray, O Lord,
I couldn't hear nobody pray, O Lord,
Oh, way down yonder by myself,
And I couldn't hear nobody pray.

The most sorrowful song on earth is a spiritual:

Sometimes I feel like a motherless child,
Sometimes I feel like a motherless child,
Sometimes I feel like a motherless child,
A long ways from home,
A long ways from home.

I just don't think there is anything sadder than a motherless child a long way from home.

Once on a visit to Africa, I saw a little wildebeest, a little baby wildebeest; his mother got killed. I don't remember how, but the mother was gone, and it was birthing season, so every mother needed her milk for her own. They had none to spare. And the little wildebeest was there with no mother, so he could just put the timer on; he was going to be killed, and he knew that, and that was one of the very saddest things.

To be a motherless child is to be totally, totally alone. And the highest praise you can pay to anybody is, "She is just like a mother to me," or, conversely, "She is like a daughter to me." The praise does not get any higher. The enslaved people sang, "Sometimes I feel like a motherless child." I like that "sometimes." Because it is so hopeful. It is not all the time, just "Sometimes I feel like a motherless child." That means we can make it. Because if you *always* feel like that, we're going to lose you.

◎◆◎◆◎ HOPE ◎◆◎◆◎

You had to hope for the children, you just had to—you had to hope that you could give them something or explain something. I think that it shows real strength of character that these people did not go into a deep depression. First the North finally realized that they couldn't continue with slavery. They didn't stop it because of any moral high ground. There were just too many days when you could not get any work out of enslaved people.

So, you got:

King Jesus lit the candle by the waterside,
To see the little children when they're truly baptized.
Honor! Honor! Unto the dying Lamb.

Oh, run along, children, and be baptized;
That's a mighty pretty meeting by the waterside.
Honor! Honor! Unto the dying Lamb.

I prayed all day, I prayed all night,
My head got sprinkled with the midnight dew.
Honor! Honor! Unto the dying Lamb.

That is a song of hope, of strength, of honor. Sometimes you are all alone. But sometimes you join in the meeting by the waterside and feel the honor, and the glory, of King Jesus.

There's plenty good room, there's plenty good room
In my Father's kingdom.
There's plenty good room, there's plenty good room
In my Father's kingdom.

My Lord has done just what He said,
Way in the kingdom:
Healed the sick and raised the dead,
Way in the kingdom.

There's plenty good room, there's plenty good room
In my Father's kingdom.
There's plenty good room, there's plenty good room
In my Father's kingdom.

One of these mornings bright and fair,
Way in the kingdom,
Going to hitch on my wings and take to the air,
Way in the kingdom.

◎◆◎◆◎ JUBILEE ◎◆◎◆◎

In the later years of slavery, there are songs of jubilation, of freedom. They are happy—they could see freedom coming.

> *I'm gonna tell you 'bout the coming of the Savior,*
> *Fare you well, fare you well,*
> *I'm gonna tell you 'bout the coming of the Savior,*
> *Fare you well, fare you well.*
> *There's a better day a-coming, fare you well, fare you well,*
> *Oh, preacher, fold your bible, fare you well, fare you well.*
>
> *In that great gettin'-up morning, fare you well, fare you well,*
> *In that great gettin'-up morning, fare you well, fare you well,*
> *In that great gettin'-up morning, fare you well, fare you well,*
> *In that great gettin'-up morning, fare you well, fare you well.*
>
> *Gabriel, blow your trumpet, fare you well, fare you well.*
> *Lord, how shall I blow it? Fare you well, fare you well.*
> *Loud as seven peals of thunder. Fare you well, fare you well.*
> *Wake the living nations. Fare you well, fare you well.*

These are happy songs, but they also include threats.

> *Didn't it rain, children?*
> *Talk about rain, O my Lord.*

Didn't it fall, didn't it fall,
Didn't it fall, my Lord, didn't it rain?

Oh, it rained forty days,
And it rained forty nights;
There was no land nowhere in sight.
God sent the angel to spread the news;
He haste his wings and away he flew
To the east, to the west,
To the north, to the south;
All day, all night, how it rained, how it rained.

◎·◎·◎ THE FIRE NEXT TIME ◎·◎·◎

The masters listening to some of these songs were not going to like them. "No more auction block for me, no more auction block for me." That comes up in many, many songs. It is always, "Before I'd be a slave, I'd be buried in my grave and go home to my Lord and be saved." In these songs there is a kind of rebellion, a defiance. As we come near to the end of slavery, as the Civil War impends, the slaves are going to sing the songs, and the "master" is going to hear them and know what he is hearing. There is no mistaking songs like "Oh, Freedom!"

> Before I'd be a slave,
> I'd be buried in my grave
> And go home to my Lord
> And be saved.

The masters would hear the Old Testament song "Didn't My Lord Deliver Daniel?" and that was a ring shout. "Deliver Daniel, deliver Daniel, / Didn't my Lord deliver Daniel, / And why not every man?" This is not just a desire for freedom, because that has always been there. This is a demand. That voice is getting bolder and bolder. When he could, the overseer would hit you for saying things like that. But when he had less control, he couldn't stop you from singing the songs.

There is a song called "Welcome Table," which goes:

I'm going to sit at the welcome table
One of these days,
One of these days, hallelujah!

It goes on: "I'm going to eat and never be hungry . . . I'm going to drink and never be thirsty . . . I'm going to work and never be tired." That all makes sense. But then in some versions it says, "God is going to set this world on fire / One of these days."

How did we get from "I'm going to sit at the welcome table" to "God is going to set this world on fire," unless we sing, "If I *don't* sit at the welcome table, then God will set this world on fire"? If . . . then—that is a demand.

God, thank goodness, is not a just God. These people knew that if God were a just God, the whole human experience would have been wiped out. God is a merciful God.

Over my head I see trouble in the air,
Over my head I see trouble in the air,
Over my head I see trouble in the air.
There must be a God somewhere.

◎◆◎◆◎ ANGER ◎◆◎◆◎

If you were a slave, it would make you crazy to be angry. To be angry, you have to do something. If two slaves wanted to marry, and she was pretty, the man would have to know that the master, or his son, was coming around. You know the man would have to say something like, "Do you think I don't know that 'Masser's' son comes down here? You think I don't know? I'm not aware? What would you like for me to say? What should I say to you? What would you like me to do? You are asking me to pay attention to a situation that is hurting me." I think anger is like that. If you have a child sold away from you, you are angry and you have this question: do you continue forward, or do you stop it here? Some people did stop it here. A lot of masters were killed—more than we know about.

One of the songs goes,

I've been 'buked and I've been scorned,
I've been 'buked and I've been scorned,
Children, I've been 'buked and I've been scorned,
Trying to make this journey all alone.

You may talk about me sure as you please,
Talk about me sure as you please,
Children, talk about me sure as you please;
Your talk will never drive me down to my knees.

Well, really it is "We've been 'buked, and we've been talked about, sure as we're born." And we still are today. But the song also says, "Ain't going to lay my religion down, / Children, ain't going to lay my religion down." And that's my grandmother, that's all of those little old ladies saying, "I'm not going to let you stop me."

Sometime after the Civil War, the anger came back. And when the anger came back, it got turned inward. Anger has not been helpful. And that is why the great black voices, such as Martin Luther King, did not turn to anger. It is not that they are not angry. The speech that everybody tries to emasculate and call the "I have a dream" speech, it wasn't the "I have a dream" speech. It was the "We are here to cash a check" speech. It is a very strong speech. But he did not go to the point of anger. King, like Frederick Douglass, stressed that, of course, you are angry. But you are not going to let that anger drive the cart. Because if you do, every time you hit a bump, somebody is going to get hurt. You have to figure out a way not to give in to anger, but to get even.

That makes a lot more sense. Getting mad doesn't solve it. Getting registered to vote helps. I'm a big fan of black people being rich. That helps.

◎◆◎◆◎ AFTER THE CIVIL WAR ◎◆◎◆◎

We know that there was a faithfulness in black couples. Right after the Civil War, one of the main reasons people hit the road was to find their husbands and wives and, if they could or had any reason to believe they could, their parents. In many cases the parents were already dead. But especially as the war was ending, many people were being sold. Wives and husbands were trying to keep track of each other. There were postings in the newspapers, which cost money. At that time, a nickel or a dime meant a lot. So if a wife would actually take a penny to post a notice saying, "I'm looking for John Williams, who is Williams's John," it was really important to her to find him. These were good people. These were strong people. They came together and they bonded and they cared.

Human memory is a wonder to me. By the late nineteenth century, people who had been enslaved twenty years earlier started to make distinctions. And so color was going to come in; hair type was going to come in; previous condition of servitude was going to come in. Now people were making distinctions. I have not seen evidence that there were tensions between the house slave and field slave. But after slavery ended, people began to say, "What did you do?" Some said, "I worked in the kitchen, so I know how to set a table." "Well, no, I worked in the field, and I also know how to set a table. The fork goes here and the knife goes there and you eat with the utensils." "No, no, no, no. Now, you have to have an oyster fork."

It really got to be that kind of imitation of the slave owners. At this point people looked down on the spirituals, which were called the "cabin songs." The great author W. E. B. Du Bois called them the "Sorrow Songs," and there is sorrow. But "cabin songs" is a better title. These were the songs that the grandmothers sang. That always takes me back to those women on the slave ships. Because the songs are their moans. And when you went to bed at night, these were the songs that you heard.

I am a graduate of Fisk University in Nashville, Tennessee. It was founded in 1866, and at first most of the students had once been slaves. By 1871, the college was running short of money and being attacked by the Ku Klux Klan. Nine students said, "Well, we can do this—we can help the school." Mr. George White, who was the musical director, said, "Well, how can you do that?" They said, "We can sing." If those nine youngsters (and two who later joined them) had said, "I need to go to school," then the rest of us would never have been educated. They sacrificed themselves.

They said, "We can sing," but everybody laughed and said, "Who wants to hear what you have to sing?" Mr. White told them, "You have to learn. I'll go with you," because you couldn't have young black people traveling around in America in 1871. There was too much racism and violence. That was just inviting somebody to kill them. Mr. White said he would accompany the students, but he told them they would have to learn the popular songs of the day. And they did, because their aim was to help the school.

They went to Murfreesboro, which was a thirty-mile walk, and they sang the songs they had learned, and everybody yawned. But they said, "We need to go on." They had Miss Ella Sheppard, and Miss Sheppard said, "I have faith; we have to go on." So they started north, and they didn't have any coats. Nashville is not warm, but it is not the North. They started north ill-clothed. But they went north. As they say, if you take one step toward God, He will take two toward you.

They finally got to Oberlin, Ohio, and they were performing these dumb songs and were not doing well. Their contributions were not even enough to keep them going. And so Miss Sheppard said—not in so many words—"If we are going to go down, let's go down doing something real." She said, "Let's stop this. We need to sing the songs that tell us who we are." And so they did.

They started to sing Nat Turner's song, "Steal Away."

Steal away, steal away, steal away to Jesus!
Steal away, steal away home,
I ain't got long to stay here.

They started to sing the spirituals, which no one had heard, and people loved hearing them. Later they sang in New York, and, fortunately, Harriet Beecher Stowe's brother, Reverend Henry Ward Beecher, was in the audience. He said, "Come to my church in Brooklyn. I'll have a concert for you." And they sang there. And it was not until they were in Brooklyn that they made enough money. Finally they had enough to be sure they could continue.

On my journey now, Mount Zion.
Well, I wouldn't take nothing, Mount Zion,
For my journey now, Mount Zion.

Their next big step was the first European tour. The Duchess of Kent took up the cause of the Jubilee Singers. She said to Queen Victoria, "You must hear them." The queen granted them an audience, and they sang for her. What she did, which was also so wonderful, was she had her painter paint them. That picture hangs in Jubilee Hall at Fisk. The group set sail for the U.S. having raised fifty thousand dollars, and that is how Jubilee Hall was built.

We did lose two of the singers, who had to bow out due to illness. But the group continued to tour. The American press, being racist and crazy, said, "Well, yeah, the British just felt really sorry for the singers, and the Irish just felt sorry because the Irish sing all those mournful songs." It was very nasty. The Jubilee Singers planned to go to Germany, where they sang for the Kaiser. Now, they had nothing in common. There was no culture in common, no image in common, no language in common.

That takes us back to the moan. Because all the Kaiser heard—he had no idea what they were saying—he heard only that moan, and it moved him. The Crown Prince actually said, "These songs as you sing them go to the heart." So the American press said, "Well, if people are enjoying it, it must be because these singers standing outside of white churches in America during slavery learned to sing from those congregations." There has been a big fight over who wrote the spirituals. And, you know, Americans need to get over that. They need to because these people didn't just write the songs; they lived them. As Marion Williams sings it, "I'm gonna live the life I sing about in my song."

Thomas A. Dorsey, who became a great gospel composer, was a jazz musician. His wife and son were killed, and he cursed the Lord. And one of his friends said, "You should not be damning the Lord; you should be praising Him." That night, Dorsey wrote "Precious Lord." It is a beautiful, beautiful song. But Dorsey, among others, was never allowed into the proper black churches. They didn't want "that kind of music" in the church.

It was all the traditional churches could do to put up with the spirituals. What they really, really wanted were the hymns. They wanted to show white people that we were cultured, proper. But, thank God, most of us said, "There is nothing to show. These people used to own us. We have nothing to show them. They need to show us something."

In the twenty-first century, the black community has finally realized, it has recognized, that we have nothing to prove. That is why the hip-hop generation is so threatening to everybody. They are not trying to prove themselves to white people. Instead they are saying, "You have to show me something good."

My generation were the dreamers. There was always bread on our tables, and I don't know anybody in my generation who ever worried about that. You were going to put bread on the table, because that's what you do. But we were not interested in building businesses the way artists are today. They are living the American dream, making money, as they should. We were singing the spirituals, and the kids are creating the hip-hop nation, but there is a connection. That is why I love them so much. I see that line linking us:

Ain't but one train runs this track;
It runs to Heaven and runs right back.

I see that that track runs from the spirituals all the way up to rap. It does. You get really wonderful things like Arrested Development doing that "Raining Revolution." But even at that, we all miss Tupac Shakur. The hip-hop community has been turned a bit. It started out to tell the truth, and then it slid into exaggeration. So we went from a legitimate story to a braggadocio, which has now run out, because now it's crazy, because now everybody is a player and everybody is in bed with three women, and it's like, "Oh, come on, now. Where is Tupac when we really need him?" That was a crucial assassination, and we definitely miss him, because whatever else Tupac was, he was honest, and we don't have anybody artistically as honest right now.

What I love about the hip-hop generation is what I've loved about my enslaved ancestors: they found a way to stay sane, and they said, "I'm not going to let you stop me." There is a line in the black community from the time of the slaves to now. For example, the funeral of Emmett Till, the fourteen-year-old boy who was murdered in Mississippi in 1955, was the largest civil rights gathering until the March on Washington. Some fifty thousand walked by the casket. Mahalia Jackson sang a song for his mother, "Pilgrim of Sorrow."

I am a poor pilgrim of sorrow,
Cast out in this wide world to roam.
My brothers and sisters won't own me;
They say that I'm weak and I'm poor.
But Jesus Father the Almighty
Has bade me to enter the door.

Sometimes I'm almost driven
Till I know not where to roam.

I've heard of a city called Heaven;
I've started to make it my home.

"I am a poor pilgrim of sorrow." That is sad. That is very sad. But it is a way to go on. We sing a song in the gospel tradition that says, "I'm glad Man didn't make me, for he would surely forsake me." Another song tells us:

The Gospel train is coming.
I hear it just at hand.
I hear them big wheels rolling
And rumbling through the land.

Won't you get on board, little children?
Get on board, little children.
Get on board, little children.
There's room for many a-more.

The hip-hop generation is getting on the train. They are not stepping off because of anyone else.

◎◆◎◆◎
SPIRITUALS TODAY AND TOMORROW
◎◆◎◆◎

I think slavery is such a key to the twenty-first century. As we are going into this new century, we must recognize it is time to embrace all of us. Whatever America is, America is the "new." It is the possibility of embracing yourself and recreating yourself. So then why are we doing these old racist things? Why are we living in that place that was no good when it was the new idea and is all the worse now that it is the old one?

I do not see a downside to black Americans. All we did was clear the land, find a way to worship our God, find a way to sing a song. That song went from the work song, to the spirituals, to gospel, to blues, to musical theater, to rhythm and blues, to hip-hop. What is the downside to this story?

I'm a big futurist, and I'll always laugh because I was invited to speak to NASA a couple of years ago, and it was wonderful—it was fun. I wrote a poem that said,

We are going to Mars. We have to go to Mars.

We can go to Mars, and we have neighbors, and it is time we quit considering people on earth as aliens. Actually, I am not even sure we should consider Martians aliens. But certainly they will be different. We've got a spacecraft out there orbiting Saturn right now. I am convinced, not in any crazy way, that we will find life somewhere. There are so many moons around Saturn. There is no reason why there could not be some form of life on some of those moons. They are separated by thousands of miles.

The question is not, "Is there intelligent life in the universe," because we have some nerve to ask, "Is there intelligent life elsewhere?" The question is, "Is there intelligent life on earth?" And the other question for earth is, "How can we recognize life in space if we fail to recognize life on earth?"

These people, these enslaved Africans, are the key, because they are the only people who have been in an unknown place without landmarks who found a way to stay human and sane. If we talk about the migration of the Irish or any of the European migrations, they wanted to come: "This is America; this is where I am trying to go." No matter whether the ship was becalmed or they had troubles on the way. They knew where they were trying to go. The fact that they were going through some dark times, some dark water, was not so frightening. They had an idea, an expectation of what they would find at the end: the streets were going to be paved with gold. But the Africans knew that whatever came when they landed could not possibly be any more pleasant than it was at the beginning. And yet they found a way to raise a song, to raise their voice, and to maintain their spirit.

When we go to Mars, when we go to Jupiter, when we go to the Dark Star, somebody is going to have to sing a song. I grew up in Cincinnati, Ohio; John Glenn ultimately became my senator before I moved. I'm a big John Glenn fan, for a lot of reasons. I like courage, and I like the way he has conducted himself. But you have to recall that John Glenn was in trouble. When he went into earth orbit, we were actually not ready to have a spacecraft with a human being in it. We sent Alan Shepard up; he went up and came back down. But John went around the world.

On the way back down, John Glenn had a problem with his heat shields. And that meant that John was going to have to turn the ship himself. The computer couldn't do it. He was going to have to turn the ship, and if he could not get it to the proper angle on his own, he was going to burn up. And so Houston did the right thing. They said, "John, we have a problem."

John heard what he had to do, and he said, "OK, I can do that." They said, "Well, Godspeed." Then he started to hum. He did. He did. And it always brings tears to my eyes. That is what he did: he hummed, and you heard him. So when he was in trouble, our astronaut, he did what black women do. I am not saying black men don't, but it is what black women do. If you go into a market with black women, you go to Africa, you go to Togo, Nigeria, it doesn't matter where you go, the market is run by women. And they are humming. And John did that.

When we send people into space, we've got to make a CD. We've got to give them some righteous music, so that these people who are earthlings, who are scared, who are vulnerable, have something to strengthen them. They need the songs so when they meet that which is different, they can at least smile. I just don't believe everything is out there to kill

us. I think that we are out there to kill what we don't understand, because that is what we do here. It has got to stop.

We have to come back to the strength of those people,
those Africans, who knew this was not a good idea. But they
decided, "I am going to go through it; I am going to go
through it and make it a song." That is a wonderful story.

♦♦♦◎♦♦♦

◎ THE SONGS — COMPLETE LYRICS ◎

The spirituals appear in many versions in books, scores, and even on the Internet. Some writers aimed to capture the sound of the language originally used by enslaved people — "chillun," for example, instead of "children," or "middle ob de wheel" instead of "middle of the wheel." I prefer to use standard spelling and grammar, except in cases such as "We am climbing Jacob's ladder" where I feel that saying "We are climbing" does not capture the same feeling as "We am."

ON MY JOURNEY, MOUNT ZION

REFRAIN:
On my journey now, Mount Zion.
Well, I wouldn't take nothing, Mount Zion,
For my journey now, Mount Zion.

One day, one day, I was walking along,
Well, the elements opened and the love come down, Mount Zion.

REFRAIN

I went to the valley and I didn't go to stay.
Well, my soul got happy and I stayed all day, Mount Zion.

REFRAIN

Just talk about me, just as much as you please.
Well, I'll talk about you when I bend on my knees, Mount Zion.

FARE YOU WELL

REFRAIN:

Fare you well, fare you well, fare you well, everybody.
Fare you well, fare you well, whenever I do get a-home.

Before I'd lie in Hell one day
I'd sing and pray my soul away.

REFRAIN

I went about from door to door
And what to do I did not know.

REFRAIN

I prayed all night and all day too
And kept on praying till I come through.

REFRAIN

Jesus speaks and He speaks mighty plain,
He speaks so the people can understand.

Fare you well, fare you well,
Fare you well, whenever I do get a-home.

DONE MADE MY VOW

REFRAIN:

Done made my vow to the Lord,
And I never will turn back.
I will go,
I shall go,
To see what the end will be.

Done opened my mouth to the Lord,
And I never will turn back.
I will go,

I shall go,
To see what the end will be.

The ones who truly love the Lord
(See what the end will be.)
Will surely get their just reward.
(See what the end will be.)

REFRAIN

When every star refuses to shine,
(See what the end will be.)
I know King Jesus will be mine.
(See what the end will be.)

IF HE CHANGED MY NAME

I told Jesus it would be all right if He changed my name,
I told Jesus it would be all right if He changed my name,
I told Jesus it would be all right if He changed my name.

And He told me that I would go hungry if He changed my name,
And He told me that I would go hungry if He changed my name,
And He told me that I would go hungry if He changed my name.

He told me that the world would be against me if He changed my
    name,
He told me that the world would be against me if He changed my
    name,
He told me that the world would be against me if He changed my
    name,

But I told Jesus it would be all right if He changed my name,
I told Jesus it would be all right if He changed my name,
So I told Him it would be all right that I would go hungry
And the world would be against me if He changed my name.

CHILD OF GOD

If anybody asks you who I am, who I am, who I am,
If anybody asks you who I am,
Tell them I'm a child of God.

WATER BOY

Water boy, where are you hiding?
If you don't come right here,
I'm gonna tell your pa on you.

There ain't no hammer
That's on-a this mountain
That rings like mine, boy,
That rings like mine.

I'm gonna bust this rock, boy,
From here to the Macon,
All the way to the jail, boy,
All the way to the jail.

You Jack o' diamond,
Jack o' diamond,
Know you of old, boy,
I know you of old.

You rob-a my pocket,
Rob my pocket
Of silver and gold, boy,
Of silver and gold.

There ain't no sweat, boy,
That's on-a this mountain
That runs like mine, boy,
That runs like mine.

GOING UP TO GLORY
Dr. Andre Thomas

Sunup to sundown, picking that cotton;
Sunup to sundown, work for the master;
Sunup to sundown, chains and shackles;
No more auction block for me.

Going up to Glory,
Going up to meet my Lord,
Going up to Glory,
Going up to meet my Lord.
Saints and sinners,
Will you go
See that heavenly light?

LET US BREAK BREAD TOGETHER
Let us break bread together on our knees (on our knees),
Let us break bread together on our knees (on our knees).
When I fall on my knees with my face to the rising sun,
O Lord, have mercy on me.

Let us drink wine together on our knees (on our knees),
Let us drink wine together on our knees (on our knees).
When I fall on my knees with my face to the rising sun,
O Lord, have mercy on me.

Let us praise God together on our knees (on our knees),
Let us praise God together on our knees (on our knees).
When I fall on my knees with my face to the rising sun,
O Lord, have mercy on me.

FOLLOW THE DRINKING GOURD

Follow the drinking gourd!
Follow the drinking gourd,
For the old man is a-waiting for to carry you to freedom
If you follow the drinking gourd.

When the sun comes back and the first quail calls,
Follow the drinking gourd,
For the old man is a-waiting for to carry you to freedom
If you follow the drinking gourd.

The riverbank makes a very good road;
The dead trees will show you the way.
Left foot, peg foot traveling on,
Following the drinking gourd.

REFRAIN

The river ends between two hills
(Follow the drinking gourd);
There's another river on the other side
(Follow the drinking gourd).

REFRAIN

When the great big river meets the little river,
Follow the drinking gourd,
For the old man is a-waiting for to carry you to freedom
If you follow the drinking gourd.

THE OLD SHIP OF ZION
'Tis the old ship of Zion,
'Tis the old ship of Zion,
'Tis the old ship of Zion.
Get on board! Get on board!

❖ 74 ❖

It has landed my old mother,
It has landed my old mother,
It has landed my old mother;
Get on board! Get on board!

It will get us through the water,
It will get us through the water,
It will get us through the water;
Get on board! Get on board!

It will take us all to heaven,
It will take us all to heaven,
It will take us all to heaven;
Get on board! Get on board!

It has landed many another,
It has landed many another,
It has landed many another;
Get on board! Get on board!

TRAMPIN'
I'm trampin', trampin',
Trying to make heaven my home;
I'm trampin', trampin',
Trying to make heaven my home;
I'm trampin', trampin',
Trying to make heaven my home;
I'm trampin', trampin',
Trying to make heaven my home.

HUSH, HUSH

Hush, hush, somebody's calling my name,
Hush, hush, somebody's calling my name,
Hush, hush, somebody's calling my name,
O my Lord, O my Lord, what shall I do?

BEEN IN THE STORM SO LONG

I've been in the storm so long,
You know I've been in the storm so long,
I've been in the storm so long,
O Lord, give me more time to pray.

I am a motherless child,
Singing, I am a motherless child.
I've been in the storm so long,
O Lord, give me more time to pray.

This is a needy time,
Singing, this is a needy time.
I've been in the storm so long,
O Lord, give me more time to pray.

Lord, I need you now,
Singing, Lord, I need you now.
I've been in the storm so long,
O Lord, give me more time to pray.

My neighbors need you now,
Singing, my neighbors need you now.
I've been in the storm so long,
O Lord, give me more time to pray.

My children need you now,
Singing, my children need you now.

I've been in the storm so long,
O Lord, give me more time to pray.

Just look what a shape I'm in,
Crying, just look what a shape I'm in.
I've been in the storm so long,
O Lord, give me more time to pray.

THIS LITTLE LIGHT OF MINE
This little light of mine,
I'm gonna let it shine.
This little light of mine,
I'm gonna let it shine.
This little light of mine,
I'm gonna let it shine,
Let it shine,
Let it shine,
Let it shine!

Hide it under a bushel? No!
I'm gonna let it shine.
Hide it under a bushel? No!
I'm gonna let it shine.
Hide it under a bushel? No!
I'm gonna let it shine,
Let it shine,
Let it shine,
Let it shine!

GO IN THE WILDERNESS

Jesus calls you. Go in the wilderness,
Go in the wilderness, go in the wilderness.
Jesus calls you. Go in the wilderness
To wait upon the Lord.

Go wait upon the Lord,
Go wait upon the Lord,
Go wait upon the Lord, my God.
He takes away the sins of the world.

Jesus is waiting. Go in the wilderness,
Go in the wilderness, go in the wilderness.
All them children go in the wilderness
To wait upon the Lord.

GO DOWN, MOSES

REFRAIN:

Go down, Moses,
'Way down in Egypt's land,
Tell old Pharaoh
To let my people go.

When Israel was in Egypt's land,
Let my people go.
Oppressed so hard they could not stand,
Let my people go.

REFRAIN

"Thus spoke the Lord," bold Moses said;
Let my people go.
"If not, I'll smite your firstborn dead."
Let my people go.

No more in bondage shall they toil;
Let my people go.
Let them come out with Egypt's spoil;
Let my people go.

JOSHUA FIT THE BATTLE OF JERICHO

REFRAIN:

Joshua fit the battle of Jericho,
Jericho, Jericho.
Joshua fit the battle of Jericho,
And the walls came tumbling down.

You may talk about your king of Gideon;
You may talk about your man of Saul.
There is none like good old Joshua
At the battle of Jericho.

Up to those walls of Jericho
He marched with spear in hand.
"Go blow those ram horns," Joshua called,
"'Cause the battle is in my hands."

REFRAIN

Then the lamb, ram, sheep horns began to blow;
Trumpets began to sound.
Joshua commanded the children to shout,
And the walls came tumbling down.

That morning, Joshua fit the battle of Jericho,
Jericho, Jericho.
Joshua fit the battle of Jericho,
And the walls came tumbling down.

DIDN'T MY LORD DELIVER DANIEL?

REFRAIN:

Didn't my Lord deliver Daniel,
Deliver Daniel, deliver Daniel,
Didn't my Lord deliver Daniel,
And why not every man?

He delivered Daniel from the lion's den,
Jonah from the belly of the whale,
And the Hebrew children from the fiery furnace,
And why not every man?

REFRAIN

The moon runs down in a purple stream,
The sun forebears to shine,
And every star disappears,
King Jesus shall be mine.

REFRAIN

The wind blows east and the wind blows west;
It blows like the Judgment day,
And every poor sinner that never did pray
I'll be glad to pray that day.

REFRAIN

I set my foot on the Gospel ship
And the ship began to sail.
It landed me on Canaan's shore,
And I'll never come back anymore.

REFRAIN

EZEKIEL SAW THE WHEEL

REFRAIN:
Wheel, oh, wheel,
Wheel in the middle of a wheel;
Wheel, oh wheel,
Wheel in the middle of a wheel.

Ezekiel saw the wheel of time,
Wheel in the middle of a wheel.
Every spoke was humankind,
Wheel in the middle of a wheel.

REFRAIN

Way up yonder on the mountaintop,
Wheel in the middle of a wheel,
My Lord spoke and the chariot stopped,
Wheel in the middle of a wheel.

Ezekiel saw the wheel
Way up in the middle of the air;
Ezekiel saw the wheel
Way up in the middle of the air.

The big wheel runs by faith;
Little wheel runs by the grace of God,
Way in the middle of the air.
Oh, the big wheel runs by faith;
Little wheel runs by the grace of God.
Wheel within a wheel,
Way in the middle of the air.

REFRAIN

KUMBAYA

Kumbaya, my Lord, kumbaya,
Kumbaya, my Lord, kumbaya,
Kumbaya, my Lord, kumbaya,
O Lord, kumbaya.

Someone's singing, Lord, kumbaya,
Someone's singing, Lord, kumbaya,
Someone's singing, Lord, kumbaya,
O Lord, kumbaya.

Someone's laughing, Lord, kumbaya,
Someone's laughing, Lord, kumbaya,
Someone's laughing, Lord, kumbaya,
O Lord, kumbaya.

Someone's crying, Lord, kumbaya,
Someone's crying, Lord, kumbaya,
Someone's crying, Lord, kumbaya,
O Lord, kumbaya.

Someone's praying. Lord, kumbaya,
Someone's praying, Lord, kumbaya,
Someone's praying, Lord, kumbaya,
O Lord, kumbaya.

Someone's sleeping, Lord, kumbaya,
Someone's sleeping, Lord, kumbaya,
Someone's sleeping, Lord, kumbaya,
O Lord, kumbaya.
O Lord, kumbaya.

HE'S GOT THE WHOLE WORLD IN HIS HANDS
He's got the whole world in His hands,
He's got the whole world in His hands,
He's got the whole world in His hands,
He's got the whole world in His hands.

He's got the wind and the rain in His hands,
He's got the wind and the rain in His hands,
He's got the wind and the rain in His hands,
He's got the whole world in His hands.

He's got the tiny little baby in His hands,
He's got the tiny little baby in His hands,
He's got the tiny little baby in His hands,
He's got the whole world in His hands.

He's got you and me, brother, in His hands,
He's got you and me, brother, in His hands,
He's got you and me, brother, in His hands,
He's got the whole world in His hands.

He's got everybody here in His hands,
He's got everybody here in His hands,
He's got everybody here in His hands,
He's got the whole world in His hands.

CHILDREN, GO WHERE I SEND THEE
Children, go where I send thee.
How will I send thee?
I'm a-going to send thee
One by one,
As was the little baby born, born, born in Bethlehem.

Children, go where I send thee
How will I send thee?
I'm going to send thee
Two by two,
Two as Paul and Silas,
One as the little baby born, born, born in Bethlehem.

Three as the Hebrew children . . .

Four as the four who stood at the door . . .

Five as the Gospel preachers . . .

Six as the six who never got fixed . . .

Seven as the seven who went up in heaven . . .

Eight as the eight who stood at the gates . . .

Nine as the nine who never went behind . . .

Ten as the Ten Commandments . . .

Eleven as the eleven disciples . . .

Twelve as the twelve apostles . . .

STEAL AWAY

REFRAIN:
Steal away, steal away, steal away to Jesus!
Steal away, steal away home,
I ain't got long to stay here.

My Lord, He calls me,
He calls me by the thunder;
The trumpet sounds within my soul,
I ain't got long to stay here.

Green trees are a-bending,
Poor sinners stand a-trembling;
The trumpet sounds within my soul,
I ain't got long to stay here.

My Lord, He calls me,
He calls me by the lightning;
The trumpet sounds within my soul,
I ain't got long to stay here.

SCANDALIZED MY NAME

Well, I met my sister the other day,
Give her my right hand.
Just as soon as ever my back was turned,
She took and scandalized my name.
Do you call that a sister?
No, no! You call that a sister?
No, no! Scandalized my name.

Well, I met my brother the other day,
Give him my right hand.
Just as soon as ever my back was turned,
He took and scandalized my name.
Do you call that a brother?
No, no! You call that a brother?
No, no! Scandalized my name.

Well, I met my preacher the other day,
Give him my right hand.
Just as soon as ever my back was turned,
He took and scandalized my name.

Do you call that a preacher?
No, no! You call that a preacher?
No, no! Scandalized my name.

WHEN I CAN READ MY TITLE CLEAR
Isaac Watts (1674–1748)

REFRAIN:
When I can read my title clear to mansions in the skies,
I bid farewell to every fear and wipe my weeping eyes,
And wipe my weeping eyes, and wipe my weeping eyes.
I bid farewell to every fear and wipe my weeping eyes.

Should earth against my soul engage and hellish darts be hurled,
Then I can smile at Satan's rage and face a frowning world,
And face a frowning world, and face a frowning world.
Then I can smile at Satan's rage and face a frowning world.

REFRAIN

Let cares like a wild deluge come and storms of sorrow fall!
May I but safely reach my home, my God, my heaven, my All;
My God, my heaven, my All; my God, my heaven, my All.
May I but safely reach my home, my God, my heaven, my All.

REFRAIN

There shall I bathe my weary soul in seas of heavenly rest,
And not a wave of trouble roll across my peaceful breast,
Across my peaceful breast, across my peaceful breast,
And not a wave of trouble roll across my peaceful breast.

AIN'T GONNA LET NOBODY TURN ME 'ROUND

Ain't gonna let nobody turn me 'round,
Turn me 'round, turn me 'round,
Ain't gonna let nobody turn me 'round.
I'm gonna keep on walking, keep on talking,
Going up to Canaan's land.

Ain't gonna let segregation turn me 'round,
Turn me 'round, turn me 'round,
Ain't gonna let segregation turn me 'round.
I'm gonna keep on walking, keep on talking,
Marching up to freedom land.

Ain't gonna let no fire hose turn me 'round,
Turn me 'round, turn me 'round,
Ain't gonna let no fire hose turn me 'round.
I'm gonna keep on walking, keep on talking,
Marching up to freedom land.

Ain't gonna let no jailhouse turn me 'round,
Turn me 'round, turn me 'round,
Ain't gonna let no jailhouse turn me 'round,
I'm gonna keep on walking, keep on talking,
Marching up to freedom land.

Ain't gonna let no police dogs turn me 'round,
Turn me 'round, turn me 'round,
Ain't gonna let no police dogs turn me 'round.
I'm gonna keep on walking, keep on talking,
Marching up to freedom land.

ALL GOD'S CHILDREN

I got a robe, you got a robe,
All God's children got a robe.
When I get to Heaven I'm going to put on my robe,
I'm going to shout all over God's Heaven.

Heaven, Heaven,
Everybody talking 'bout Heaven ain't going there;
Heaven, Heaven,
I'm going to shout all over God's Heaven.

I got-a wings, you got-a wings,
All God's children got-a wings.
When I get to Heaven I'm going to put on my wings,
I'm going to fly all over God's Heaven,

Heaven, Heaven,
Everybody talking 'bout Heaven ain't going there;
Heaven, Heaven,
I'm going to fly all over God's Heaven.

I got a harp, you got a harp,
All God's children got a harp.
When I get to Heaven I'm going to take up my harp,
I'm going to play all over God's Heaven.

Heaven, Heaven,
Everybody talking 'bout Heaven ain't going there.
Heaven, Heaven,
I'm going to play all over God's Heaven.

I got shoes, you got shoes,
All God's children got shoes.
When I get to Heaven I'm going to put on my shoes,
I'm going to walk all over God's Heaven.

Heaven, Heaven,
Everybody talking 'bout Heaven ain't going there.
Heaven, Heaven,
I'm going to walk all over God's Heaven.

WE AM CLIMBING JACOB'S LADDER
We am climbing
Jacob's ladder,
We am climbing
Jacob's ladder,
We am climbing
Jacob's ladder,
Soldiers of the cross.

Every round goes
Higher, higher,
Every round goes
Higher, higher,
Every round goes
Higher, higher,
Soldiers of the cross.

WILL THE CIRCLE BE UNBROKEN?
REFRAIN:
Will the circle be unbroken?
By and by, Lord, by and by,
There's a better home a-waiting
In the sky, Lord, in the sky.

I was standing by my front door
On a cold and cloudy day

When I saw the hearse come rolling
To carry my mother away.

REFRAIN

Undertaker, undertaker,
Undertaker, please go slow,
'Cause this lady that you're hauling,
Oh, I hate to see her go.

REFRAIN

I did follow close behind her,
Trying to haul her bane with prayer,
But I could not hold my sorrow
When they laid her in the grave.

REFRAIN

WERE YOU THERE?

Were you there when they crucified my Lord?
Were you there when they crucified my Lord?
Oh! Sometimes it causes me to tremble, tremble, tremble.
Were you there when they crucified my Lord?

Were you there when they nailed him to the tree?
Were you there when they nailed him to the tree?
Oh! Sometimes it causes me to tremble, tremble, tremble.
Were you there when they nailed him to the tree?

Were you there when they laid him in the tomb?
Were you there when they laid him in the tomb?
Oh! Sometimes it causes me to tremble, tremble, tremble.
Were you there when they laid him in the tomb?

Were you there when God raised him from the tomb?
Were you there when God raised him from the tomb?
Oh! Sometimes it causes me to tremble, tremble, tremble.
Were you there when God raised him from the tomb?

LORD, I WANT TO BE A CHRISTIAN

Lord, I want to be a Christian in my heart, in my heart,
Lord, I want to be a Christian in my heart.
In my heart, in my heart,
Lord, I want to be a Christian in my heart.

Lord, I want to be more loving in my heart, in my heart,
Lord, I want to be more loving in my heart.
In my heart, in my heart,
Lord, I want to be more loving in my heart.

Lord, I want to be more holy in my heart, in my heart,
Lord, I want to be more holy in my heart.
In my heart, in my heart,
Lord, I want to be more holy in my heart.

Lord, I want to be like Jesus in my heart, in my heart,
Lord, I want to be like Jesus in my heart.
In my heart, in my heart,
Lord, I want to be like Jesus in my heart.

HE NEVER SAID A MUMBLING WORD

They crucified my Lord,
Not a word, not a word, not a word.
They crucified my Lord,
Not a word, not a word, not a word.
They crucified my Lord,

But He never said a mumbling word,
Not a word, not a word, not a word.

They nailed Him to a tree. . . .

They pierced Him in the side. . . .

The blood came trickling down. . . .

He bowed His head and died. . . .

Wasn't that a pity and a shame?
Not a word, not a word, not a word.
Wasn't that a pity and a shame?
Not a word, not a word, not a word.
They crucified my Lord,
But He never said a mumbling word,
Not a word, not a word, not a word.

GIVE ME JESUS
I heard my mother say,
I heard my mother say,
I heard my mother say,
"Give me Jesus."

REFRAIN:
Give me Jesus,
Give me Jesus.
You may have all this world;
Give me Jesus.

At dark midnight was my cry,
Dark midnight was my cry,
Dark midnight was my cry,
"Give me Jesus."

In the morning when I rise,
In the morning when I rise,
In the morning when I rise,
Give me Jesus.

And when I come to die,
And when I come to die,
And when I come to die,
Give me Jesus.

AIN'T GOT TIME TO DIE
Hall Johnson

Lord, I keep so busy praising my Jesus,
Keep so busy praising my Jesus,
Keep so busy praising my Jesus,
Ain't got time to die.

'Cause when I'm healing the sick,
When I'm healing the sick,
When I'm healing the sick,
I'm praising my Jesus,
Ain't got time to die.

'Cause it takes all of my time,
It takes all of my time,
It takes all of my time
To praise my Jesus,
Ain't got time to die.

If I don't praise Him,
If I don't praise Him,
If I don't praise Him,
The rocks are going to cry out,
"Glory and honor! Glory and honor!"
Ain't got time to die.

'Cause when I'm feeding the poor,
When I'm feeding the poor,
When I'm feeding the poor,
I'm working for the Kingdom,
Ain't got time to die.

Lord, I keep so busy working for the Kingdom,
Keep so busy working for the Kingdom,
Keep so busy working for the Kingdom,
Ain't got time to die.

I COULDN'T HEAR NOBODY PRAY

And I couldn't hear nobody pray, O Lord,
I couldn't hear nobody pray, O Lord,
Oh, way down yonder by myself,
And I couldn't hear nobody pray.
In the valley,
I couldn't hear nobody pray.
On my knees,
I couldn't hear nobody pray.
With my burden,
I couldn't hear nobody pray.
And my Savior,
I couldn't hear nobody pray, O Lord,
Oh, way down yonder by myself,
And I couldn't hear nobody pray.

SOMETIMES I FEEL LIKE A MOTHERLESS CHILD

Sometimes I feel like a motherless child,
Sometimes I feel like a motherless child,
Sometimes I feel like a motherless child,
A long ways from home,
A long ways from home.

True believer!
A long ways from home,
A long ways from home.

Sometimes I feel like I'm almost gone,
Sometimes I feel like I'm almost gone,
Sometimes I feel like I'm almost gone,
Way up in the heavenly land.

True believer!
Way up in the heavenly land,
Way up in the heavenly land.

HONOR! HONOR!

King Jesus lit the candle by the waterside,
To see the little children when they're truly baptized.
Honor! Honor! Unto the dying Lamb.

Oh, run along, children, and be baptized;
That's a mighty pretty meeting by the waterside.
Honor! Honor! Unto the dying Lamb.

I prayed all day, I prayed all night,
My head got sprinkled with the midnight dew.
Honor! Honor! Unto the dying Lamb.

PLENTY GOOD ROOM

REFRAIN:

There's plenty good room, there's plenty good room,
In my Father's kingdom.
There's plenty good room, there's plenty good room,
In my Father's kingdom.

My Lord has done just what He said,
Way in the kingdom:
Healed the sick and raised the dead,
Way in the kingdom.

REFRAIN

One of these mornings bright and fair,
Way in the kingdom,
Going to hitch on my wings and take to the air,
Way in the kingdom.

REFRAIN

When I was a mourner just like you,
Way in the kingdom,
I prayed and I prayed till I came through,
Way in the kingdom.

REFRAIN

Come on, mourner, make a bound,
Way in the kingdom;
The Lord will meet you on halfway ground,
Way in the kingdom.

REFRAIN

IN THAT GREAT GETTIN'-UP MORNING

I'm gonna tell you 'bout the coming of the Savior,
Fare you well, fare you well,
I'm gonna tell you 'bout the coming of the Savior,
Fare you well, fare you well.
There's a better day a-coming, fare you well, fare you well,
Oh, preacher, fold your Bible, fare you well, fare you well,

Prayermaker, pray no more, fare you well, fare you well,
For the last soul's converted, fare you well, fare you well.

That time shall be no longer, fare you well, fare you well,
For Judgment Day is coming, fare you well, fare you well.

Then you hear the sinner saying, fare you well, fare you well,
Down I'm rolling, down I'm rolling, fare you well, fare you well.

REFRAIN:
In that great gettin'-up morning, fare you well, fare you well,
In that great gettin'-up morning, fare you well, fare you well,
In that great gettin'-up morning, fare you well, fare you well,
In that great gettin'-up morning, fare you well, fare you well.

The Lord spoke to Gabriel, fare you well, fare you well.
Go look behind the altar, fare you well, fare you well.
Take down a silver trumpet, fare you well, fare you well.
Blow your trumpet, Gabriel, fare you well, fare you well.

Lord, how shall I blow it? Fare you well, fare you well.
Blow it right calm and easy. Fare you well, fare you well.
Do not alarm my people. Fare you well, fare you well.
Tell them to come to the Judgment. Fare you well, fare you well.

Gabriel, blow your trumpet, fare you well, fare you well.
Lord, how shall I blow it? Fare you well, fare you well.

Loud as seven peals of thunder. Fare you well, fare you well.
Wake the living nations. Fare you well, fare you well.

Then you'll see that fork of lightning, fare you well, fare you well,
Then you'll hear that rumbling thunder, fare you well, fare you well,
Then you'll see them stars a-falling, fare you well, fare you well,
Then you'll see the world on fire, fare you well, fare you well.

Then you'll see them sinners rising, fare you well, fare you well,
See them marching home for heaven, fare you well, fare you well.
Farewell, poor sinners, fare you well, fare you well,
Farewell, poor sinners, fare you well, fare you well.

REFRAIN

DIDN'T IT RAIN?
Didn't it rain, children?
Talk about rain, O my Lord.
Didn't it fall, didn't it fall,
Didn't it fall, my Lord, didn't it rain?

Oh, it rained forty days,
And it rained forty nights;
There was no land nowhere in sight.
God sent the angel to spread the news;
He haste his wings and away he flew
To the east, to the west,
To the north, to the south;
All day, all night, how it rained, how it rained.

OH, FREEDOM!

REFRAIN:

Oh, freedom! Oh, freedom!
Oh, freedom over me!
Before I'd be a slave,
I'd be buried in my grave
And go home to my Lord
And be saved.

Oh, what preaching! Oh, what preaching!
Oh, what preaching over me, over me.
Oh, what preaching! Oh, what preaching!
Oh, what preaching over me.
Oh, what mourning! . . .

Oh, what singing! . . .

Oh, what shouting! . . .

Oh, weeping Mary . . .

Doubting Thomas . . .

Oh, what sighing! . . .

REFRAIN

WELCOME TABLE

I'm going to sit at the welcome table
One of these days,
One of these days, hallelujah!

I'm going to eat and never be hungry
One of these days,
One of these days, hallelujah!

I'm going to drink and never be thirsty
One of these days,
One of these days, hallelujah!

I'm going to work and never be tired
One of these days,
One of these days, hallelujah!

I'm going to put on my long white robe
One of these days,
One of these days, hallelujah!

I'm going tell God how you treat me
One of these days,
One of these days, hallelujah!

God is going to set this world on fire
One of these days,
One of these days, hallelujah!

I'm going to sit at the welcome table
One of these days,
One of these days, hallelujah!
I'm going to sit at the welcome table
One of these days.

OVER MY HEAD

Over my head I hear music in the air,
Over my head I hear music in the air,
Over my head I hear music in the air.
There must be a God somewhere.

Over my head I hear singing in the air,
Over my head I hear singing in the air,

Over my head I hear singing in the air.
There must be a God somewhere.

Over my head I see trouble in the air,
Over my head I see trouble in the air,
Over my head I see trouble in the air.
There must be a God somewhere.

Over my head I feel gladness in the air,
Over my head I feel gladness in the air,
Over my head I feel gladness in the air.
There must be a God somewhere.

Over my head I see angels in the air,
Over my head I see angels in the air,
Over my head I see angels in the air.
There must be a God somewhere.

'BUKED AND SCORNED

I've been 'buked and I've been scorned,
I've been 'buked and I've been scorned,
Children, I've been 'buked and I've been scorned,
Trying to make this journey all alone.

You may talk about me sure as you please,
Talk about me sure as you please,
Children, talk about me sure as you please;
Your talk will never drive me down to my knees.

Ain't gonna lay my religion down,
Ain't gonna lay my religion down,
Children, ain't gonna lay my religion down,
Ain't gonna lay my religion down.

Jesus died to set me free,
Jesus died to set me free,
Children, Jesus died to set me free,
Nailed to that cross on Calvary.

EVERY TIME I FEEL THE SPIRIT
REFRAIN:
Every time I feel the spirit moving in my heart, I will pray,
Every time I feel the spirit moving in my heart, I will pray.

Upon the mountain my God spoke,
Out of God's mouth came fire and smoke.
Looked all around me; looked so fine,
I asked God if all was mine.

REFRAIN

Ain't but one train runs this track;
It runs to Heaven and runs right back.
Saint Peter, waiting at the gate,
Says, "Come on, sinner, don't be late."

REFRAIN

PILGRIM OF SORROW
I am a poor pilgrim of sorrow,
Cast out in this wide world to roam.
My brothers and sisters won't own me;
They say that I'm weak and I'm poor.
But Jesus Father the Almighty
Has bade me to enter the door.

Sometimes I'm almost driven
Till I know not where to roam.
I've heard of a city called Heaven;
I've started to make it my home.

GOSPEL TRAIN

The Gospel train is coming.
I hear it just at hand.
I hear them big wheels rolling
And rumbling through the land.

REFRAIN:

Won't you get on board, little children?
Get on board, little children.
Get on board, little children.
There's room for many a-more.

That Gospel train is coming.
It's coming around the curve.
She's loosened all her steam and brakes;
She's straining every nerve.

REFRAIN

The fare is cheap and all can go.
The rich and poor are there.
No second class aboard this train;
No difference in the fare.

REFRAIN

⊙ GLOSSARY OF NAMES AND TERMS ⊙

ABIGAIL ADAMS (1744–1818): Although she was both the wife of the second President (John Adams) and mother of the sixth (John Quincy Adams), Abigail Adams is now best known for being a thoughtful, intelligent, forthright person herself. In a famous 1776 letter to her husband, she urged him not to neglect the rights of women.

KATHLEEN BATTLE (1948–): A five-time Grammy Award winner, Battle is one of the world's best-known singers of opera and classical music. She has also recorded albums of spirituals and contemporary music.

HENRY WARD BEECHER (1813–1887): The brother of Harriet and an influential minister. Rev. Beecher opened his church to the Fisk Singers, later to be known as the Fisk Jubilee Singers, who were touring to raise funds to save Fisk University, the first coeducational college established for the freedmen and women.

JAMES CONE (1938–): A minister and theologian, Cone is known for his deep understanding of the relationship between African-American life and Christian faith.

THOMAS A. DORSEY (1899–1993): Started out as a blues musician and later became a great gospel composer.

FREDERICK DOUGLASS (1818–1895): Escaped enslavement, joined the abolitionist movement, and became one of its greatest spokespersons. Traveled abroad and counseled President Abraham Lincoln to sign the Emancipation Proclamation.

W. E. B. DU BOIS (1868–1963): American scholar whose findings on the Atlantic slave trade are still the standard by which other scholarly works are judged. One of the founding members of the National Association for the Advancement of Colored People, he edited *The Crisis* magazine, which is still published monthly. Du Bois migrated to Ghana, where he worked on the *Encyclopedia Africana,* which was completed by Henry Louis Gates and Anthony Appiah. Du Bois died peacefully, after almost a century of life, the night before the 1963 March on Washington.

FUGITIVE SLAVE ACT (1850): The Act essentially made all Americans slave owners because it required the return of any runaway under the penalty of confiscation of property and jail. Because of the attention it paid to escaping slaves, the Act can be seen as an admission by the slaveholding South that the enslaved were running away in large numbers.

ZORA NEALE HURSTON (ca 1891–1960): Best known for her novel *Their Eyes Were Watching God,* Hurston not only invented worlds in her imagination; she was also a trained anthropologist and a diligent researcher of African-American life.

"I HAVE A DREAM": In this speech, given at the March on Washington on August 28, 1963, Dr. Martin Luther King Jr. began by speaking of the debt America owed to black people. He then painted a vivid word picture of an integrated nation in which the children of all races could live together. It is considered one of the greatest speeches in American history.

MAHALIA JACKSON (1911–1972): The world's greatest gospel singer, she opened up concert halls for this music. She sang at the March on Washington. And, no, it didn't rain, children.

HALL JOHNSON (1888–1970): Although he was trained in classical music, fluent in German and French, a skilled composer of music for the theater, and active in Hollywood films, Johnson's greatest attachment was to the spirituals. He wrote "Ain't Got Time to Die" in the style of the songs he knew so well.

JAMES WELDON JOHNSON (1871–1938): Truly a Renaissance man, he cowrote with his brother, Rosamond, the song "Lift Every Voice and Sing," known as the "Negro National Anthem"; was ambassador to Mexico; was one of the founding fathers of the Harlem Renaissance; wrote "I'm Just Wild About Harry," which Truman used as his campaign song; wrote *The Autobiography of an Ex-Colored Man,* which is still in print, among many other contributions.

MIDDLE PASSAGE: Slave-trading routes formed a transatlantic triangle: Slave traders first sailed from Europe carrying goods valued in Africa. The second leg of their route—the Middle Passage—involved taking people purchased in Africa to the Americas. The traders then returned to Europe with products from the Americas. This harsh experience of being treated as property was designed to turn individuals into slaves.

BERNICE JOHNSON REAGON (1942–): A founder of the group Sweet Honey in the Rock and of the Smithsonian Institution's Program in African American Culture, she is known equally as a scholar and an artist.

PAUL ROBESON (1898–1976): The son of a slave who escaped to freedom, Robeson went to Rutgers University, where he was a two-time football All-American. He achieved greatness, though, as a singer and actor who sought always to share the music of all peoples with the entire world. His deep bass voice is unmistakable, and thrilling to hear.

SHARECROPPING: Even after the Civil War, many former slaves had no choice but to work on plantations. They were paid a share of the value of the crops they picked but were also charged rent, so they were always in debt. Since workers were paid by the weight of crops they picked, owners preferred them to pick cotton when it was dry and weighed less.

STONO UPRISING (September 1739): A violent clash near the Stono River in South Carolina between escaping slaves and whites that left some sixty people dead. It was the largest slave rebellion before the American Revolution. After the clash, the lives of slaves in the colony became much more difficult.

HARRIET BEECHER STOWE (1811–1896): Author of *Uncle Tom's Cabin,* the single most important anti-slavery book at that time. When President Abraham Lincoln met her, he said, "So you're the little woman who started this big war!"

HARRIET TUBMAN (ca 1820–1913): Leader and organizer of the Underground Railroad, she helped more than two hundred enslaved Africans escape to freedom. She also worked as a spy for the Union Army during the Civil War and earned an army pension for her efforts. She died peacefully on her front porch near Buffalo, New York.

NAT TURNER (1800–1831): An enslaved African, he led a great rebellion against the planters.

UNDERGROUND RAILROAD: The set of personal connections through which African Americans escaped from slavery. Although there were "conductors" who tried to help people escape, and homes that provided harbor and safety along the way, this was not a highly organized system with a single center. Instead slaves made their way as well as they could, learning from others as they went along.

PHILLIS WHEATLEY (1753–1784): African-born youngster sold into American slavery. She remembered Africa, but her poems reflected her acceptance of her new land. She earned her freedom through her talent, becoming one of the first published women in America.

MARION WILLIAMS (1927–1994): In a career that took her throughout America, the Caribbean, and Europe, Williams spread both the sound and word of spirituals and of Gospel. She starred in the play *Black Nativity*, by Langston Hughes. Her most famous recording was of "How I Got Over."

Spirituals were sung in fields, at services, and in homes long before they were first written down. Surely they were sung in different ways at different times. It was only generations later, as singers, musicians, and composers recalled songs learned from their parents and grandparents, that the "official" versions were set down. As a result, tracing the sources of many spirituals is not easy. While the musical arrangements printed in books and scores are usually credited to their composers, the texts are not as clear-cut. The original song may be "traditional," while a specific printed version is credited to its "author." It is not even as simple as that sounds, since some fine composers later wrote spirituals in the style of traditional favorites or created new songs by mixing and matching parts of the spirituals they recalled hearing.

Sources used for tracing the lyrics printed in this book included:

The Books of American Negro Spirituals: Including the Book of American Negro Spirituals and the Second Book of Negro Spirituals, compiled by James Weldon Johnson and J. Rosamond Johnson (reprint ed. New York: Dover Press, 1977). These two pioneering collections are the classics of the field.

African American Heritage Hymnal (Chicago: Gia Publications, 2001). The product of years of effort, this book was created by a team of scholars, theologians, and pastors.

Songs of Zion (Nashville, Tenn.: Abingdon Press, 1981). Another team effort, in this instance from the United Methodist Church, this collection includes historical essays as well as songs and scores.

Dr. Arthur C. Jones and Dr. Andre Thomas were extremely helpful in filling in gaps, as were the highly informed contributors to the Mudcat listserv. (If you join Mudcat, which is free of charge, you can search their permathread on spirituals, which has many marvelous links to texts, lyrics, and the history of spirituals.)

Those interested in the spirituals will also find Arthur C. Jones's *Wade in the Water: The Wisdom of the Spirituals* (Maryknoll, New York: Orbis, 1999) very useful.

"Ain't Got Time to Die" was written by Hall Johnson. Johnson knew the spirituals extremely well, but the song is his own creation.

"Going Up to Glory" is by Dr. Andre Thomas, who graciously gave us permission to use the lyrics. "I was just calling upon childhood experience with the words," he explains. "The beginning is from a field holler called 'Sunup to Sundown.' It also includes a reference to the spiritual 'Goin' Up,' as well as additional text by me. The tune for the words," he says, "is totally mine."

"Water Boy" originated as a song sung by prisoners. It may well date back to slavery, but there is no certainty of that. The song is sung by men and women in need of relief. I look at this song as being handed down to the prisoners from the enslaved and not originating with the prisoners. Just as during the civil rights movement songs were revived and new verses added, this song has arisen when needed. Of course, there are no more chain gangs, so a lot of songs that came and were revived during that era are no longer with us. Think of Sam Cooke's "Chain Gang," a fifties hit, and Nina Simone's rendition of Oscar Brown's "Chain Gang," also a hit. "Water boy, where are you hiding? / If you don't come right here, / Gonna tell your ma on you" is the way I first heard it.

Tracing the story of these songs is a fascinating historical challenge. If readers find sources that we have inadvertently missed, please let us know so that we may correct future editions.

◎ RECOMMENDED RECORDINGS ◎

Here are some of my favorite recordings of spirituals and gospel music:

Marion Anderson. *He's Got the Whole World in His Hands*. RCA 61960.

Kathleen Battle. *So Many Stars*. Sony 68473.

Kathleen Battle and Jessye Norman. *Spirituals in Concert*. Deutsche Grammophon 429790.

Kathleen Battle, Jessye Norman, and Florence Quivar. *Great American Spirituals, Volume 9*. Angel 64669. A rare opportunity to hear Florence Quivar perform the "Lord's Prayer."

James Cleveland and the Angelic Choir. *I Stood on the Banks of the Jordan*. Savoy 14096. *Peace Be Still*. Savoy 14076.

The Fisk University Jubilee Singers. *In Bright Mansions*. Curb 78762. *Volume 2*. Document DOCD-5534. *Volume 3*. Document DOCD-5535.

Charlie Haden and Hank Jones. *Steal Away: Spirituals, Hymns, and Folk Songs*. Polygram 527249.

Barbara Hendricks and the Moses Hogan Singers. *Give Me Jesus*. EMI Classics 56788.

The Moses Hogan Chorale. *Negro Spirituals*. EMI Classics 63305.

Leontyne Price. *The Essential Leontyne Price: Spirituals, Hymns, and Sacred Songs*. RCA 68157.

Sweet Honey in the Rock. *Sacred Ground*. Earthbeat 42580.

◎ INDEX OF SONG TITLES ◎

◎ INDEX ◎